CONFIGURING ACCOUNTS PAYABLE WITHIN DYNAMICS AX 2012

BY MURRAY FIFE

Preface

What You Need For This Guide

All the examples shown in this blueprint were done with the Microsoft Dynamics AX 2012 virtual machine image that was downloaded from the Microsoft CustomerSource or PartnerSource site. If you don't have your own installation of Microsoft Dynamics AX 2012, you can also use the images found on the Microsoft Learning Download Center or deployed through Lifecycle Services. The following list of software from the virtual image was leveraged within this guide:

- Microsoft Dynamics AX 2012 R3

Even though all the preceding software was used during the development and testing of the recipes in this book, they may also work on earlier versions of the software with minor tweaks and adjustments, and should also work on later versions without any changes.

Errata

Although we have taken every care to ensure the accuracy of our content, mistakes do happen. If you find a mistake in one of our books—maybe a mistake in the text or the code—we would be grateful if you would report this to us. By doing so, you can save other readers from frustration and help us improve subsequent versions of this book. If you find any errata, please report them by emailing editor@dynamicsaxcompanions.com.

Piracy

Piracy of copyright material on the Internet is an ongoing problem across all media. If you come across any illegal copies of our works, in any form, on the Internet, please provide us with the location address or website name immediately so that we can pursue a remedy.

Please contact us at legal@dynamicsaxcompanions.com with a link to the suspected pirated material.

We appreciate your help in protecting our authors, and our ability to bring you valuable content.

Questions

You can contact us at help@dynamicsaxcompanions.com if you are having a problem with any aspect of the book, and we will do our best to address it.

Table Of Contents

CONFIGURING PAYABLES INVOICE JOURNAL APPROVALS (Ctd)

INTRODUCTION

The Accounts Payable area is one of the three foundation financial modules within Dynamics AX that you will want to set up. It not only allows you to manage all of your vendor information, post your invoices, and make in your payments, but also allows you to manage approval workflows, and much more.

It's not hard to configure either and this book is designed to give you step by step instructions to show you how to configure the payables area, and also how some of the basic transactions work to get you up and running and working with your vendors.

CONFIGURING ACCOUNTS PAYABLE CONTROLS

Before we start adding vendors and creating invoices within the Accounts Payable module of Dynamics AX, there are a couple of codes and controls that need to be configured so that everything else later on in the book will run smoothly. In this section we will walk through everything that you need to set up to get the basic Accounts Payable features working.

Configuring Payables Journal Names

Everything you do within the Payables area of Dynamics AX is controlled through Journals. So it makes sense that the very first thing that we need to do is to configure some default Journal Names that we can then start using for our journal postings. We will want to create two new Journals right now for Vendor Payments and also the Invoice Journals.

Configuring Payables Journal Names

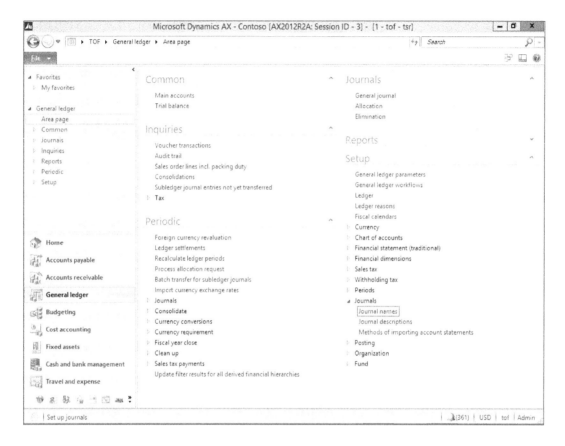

To do this, click on the **Journal Names** menu item within the **Journals** folder of the **Setup** group within the **General Ledger** area page.

Configuring Payables Journal Names

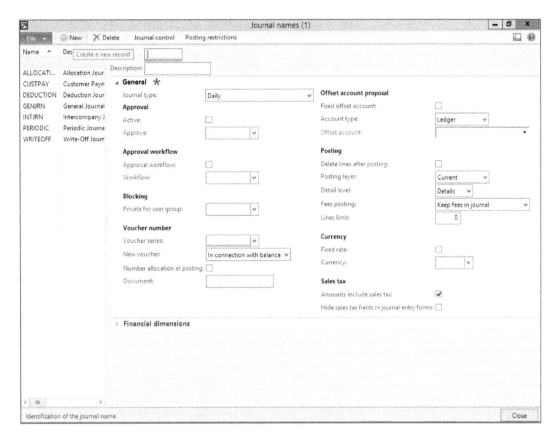

When the **Journal Names** maintenance form is displayed, click on the **New** button in the menu bar to create a new record.

Configuring Payables Journal Names

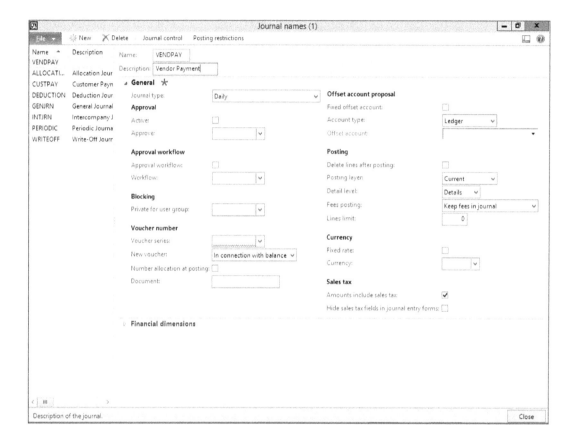

The first journal that we will create is for Vendor Payments. To do this, set the **Name** to **VENDPAY** and the **Description** to **Vendor Payment.**

Configuring Payables Journal Names

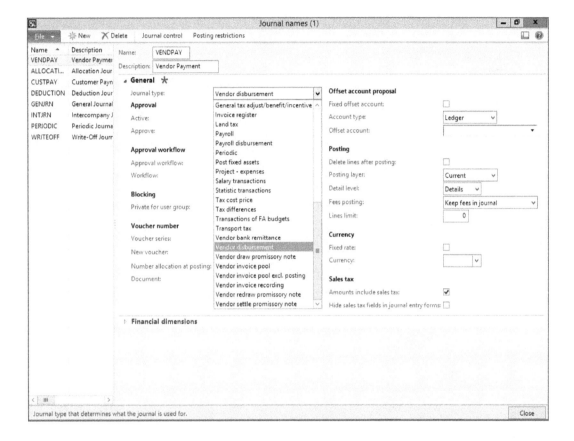

Then from the **Journal Type** dropdown list, select the **Vendor Disbursement** option.

Configuring Payables Journal Names

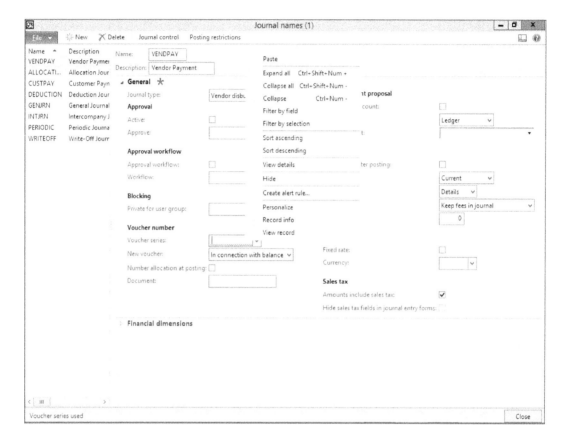

Nest we need to create a **Number Sequence** for the journal. To do this right-mouse-click on the **Voucher Series** field and click on the **View Details** menu item.

Configuring Payables Journal Names

When the **Number Sequences** form is displayed, click n the **Number Sequence** button within the **New** group of the **Number Sequence** ribbon bar.

Configuring Payables Journal Names

Set the **Number Sequence Code** to **VendPay_01** and the **Name** to **Vendor Payment**.

Configuring Payables Journal Names

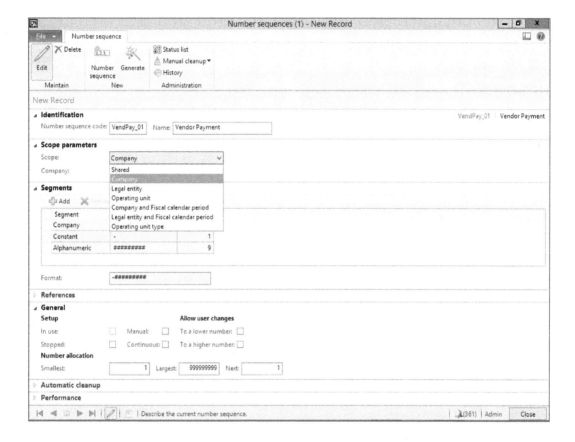

Click on the dropdown list for the **Scope** field and select the **Company value.**

Configuring Payables Journal Names

Then from the **Company** dropdown list select your company that you are using.

Configuring Payables Journal Names

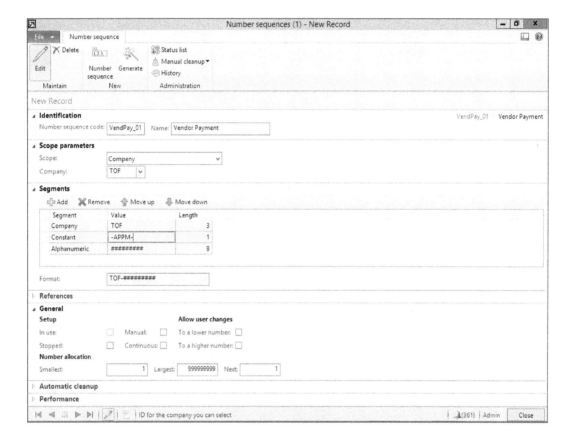

Within the **Segments** tab group, set the **Constant** segment value to **–APPM-** so that you can identify all of the Vendor Payment journals.

Configuring Payables Journal Names

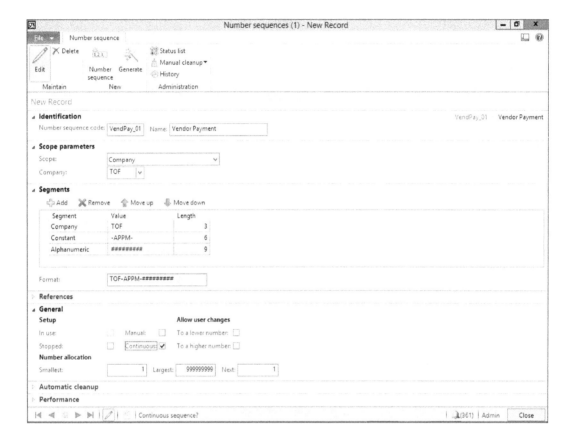

Finally check the **Continuous** flag within the **General** tab group.

When you are done, click on the **Close** button to exit from the form.

Configuring Payables Journal Names

When you return to the **Journal Names** you will now be able to select your new number sequence from the **Voucher Series** dropdown list.

Configuring Payables Journal Names

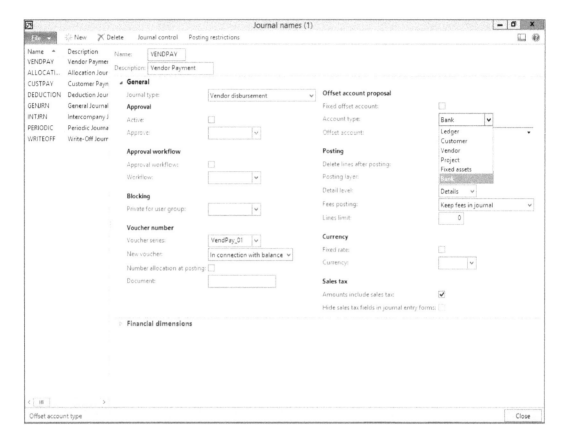

Since this is a vendor payment we will want to click on the **Account Type** field and change the value to **Bank**.

Configuring Payables Journal Names

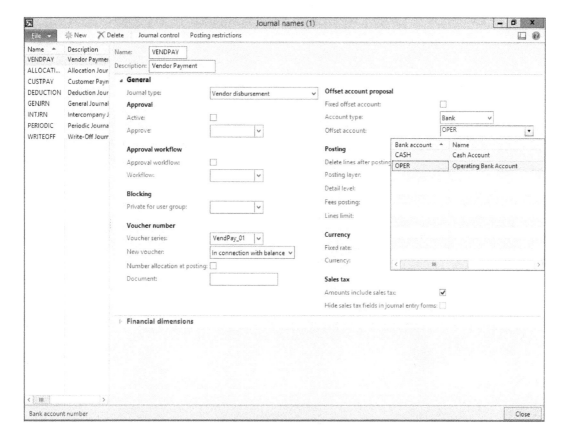

Then click on the dropdown list for the **Offset Account** and select the bank account that you want to pay the vendors from.

Configuring Payables Journal Names

Configuring Payables Journal Names

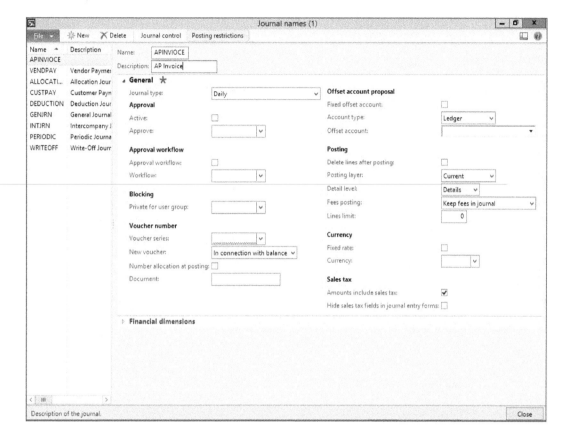

The next journal that we want to create is for the **AP Invoices**. To do this, click on the **New** button in the menu bar to create a new record and then set the **Name** to **APINVOICE** and the **Description** to **AP Invoice**.

Configuring Payables Journal Names

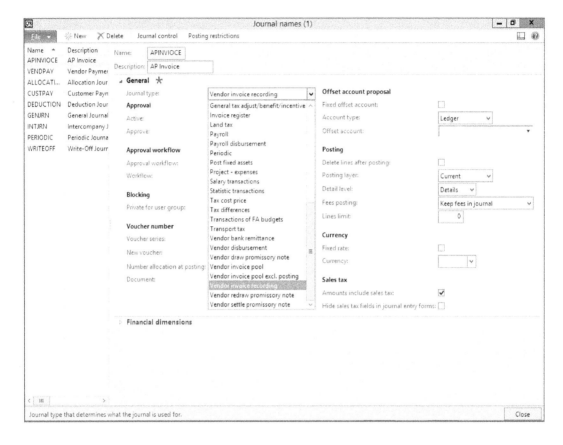

Then click on the **Journal Type** dropdown list and select the **Vendor Invoice Recording** value.

Configuring Payables Journal Names

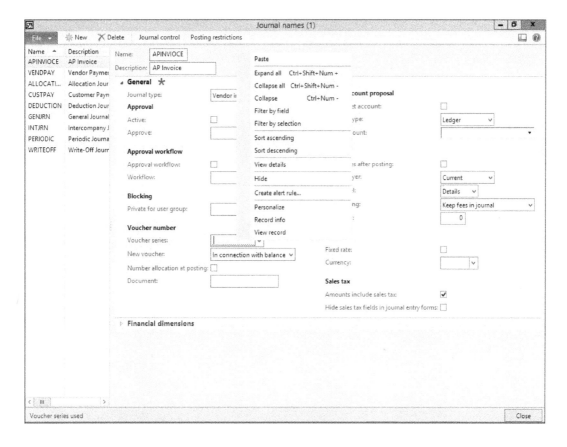

We will create a new number sequence for this journal as well by right-mouse-clicking on the **Voucher Series** field and clicking on the **View Details** menu item.

Configuring Payables Journal Names

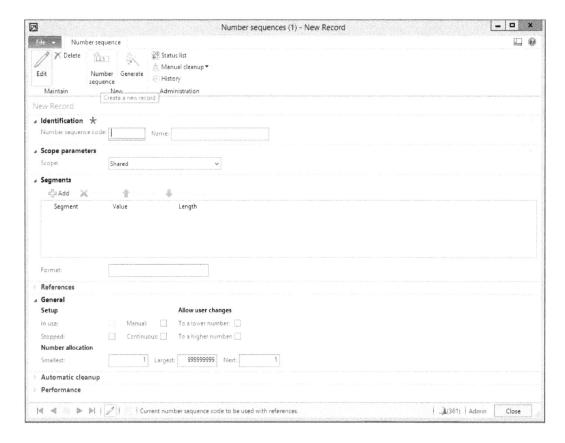

When the **Number Sequences** maintenance form is displayed, click on the **Number Sequence** button within the **New** group of the **Number Sequence** ribbon bar to create a new record.

Configuring Payables Journal Names

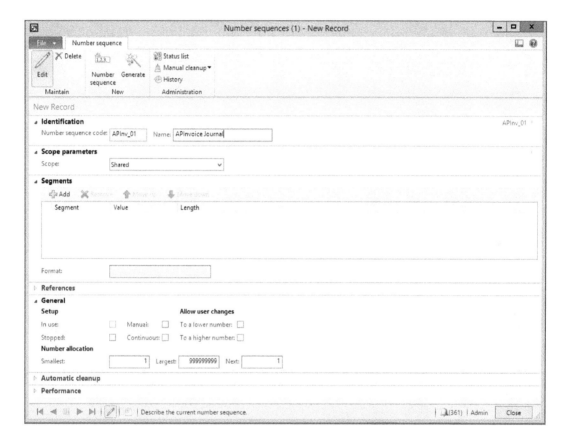

Set the **Number Sequence Code** to **APInv_01** and the **Name** to **AP Invoice Journal**.

Configuring Payables Journal Names

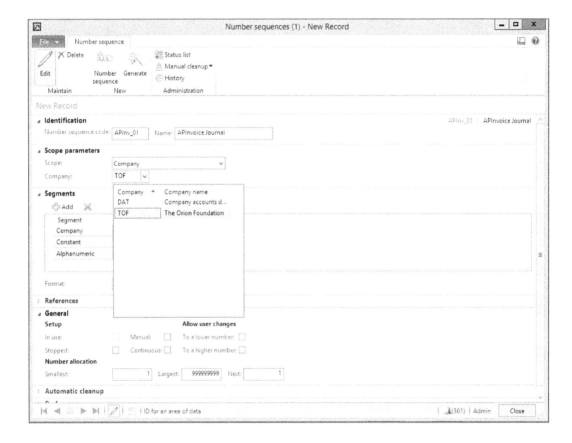

Change the **Scope** to **Company** and then click on the **Company** dropdown list and select the company that you want to assign the number sequence to.

Configuring Payables Journal Names

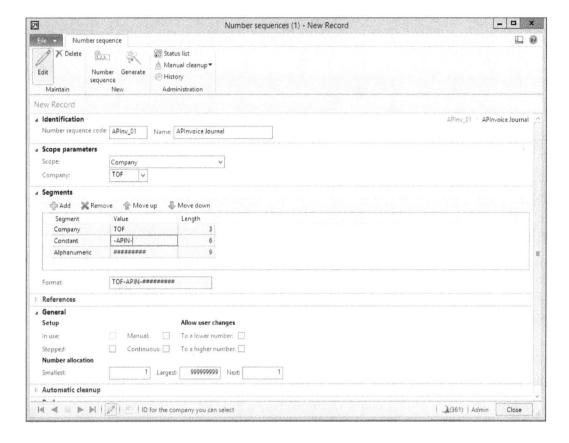

Then change the **Constant** value within the **Segments** table to **–APIN-** to uniquely identify your AP Invoice Journal journals.

Configuring Payables Journal Names

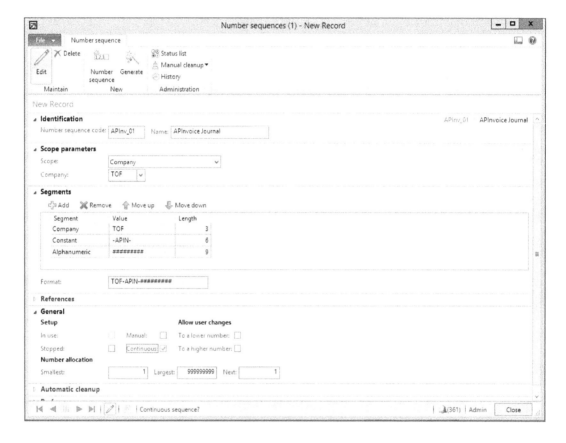

Finally, check the **Continuous** flag within the **General** tab group.

Then click on the **Close** button to exit from the form.

Configuring Payables Journal Names

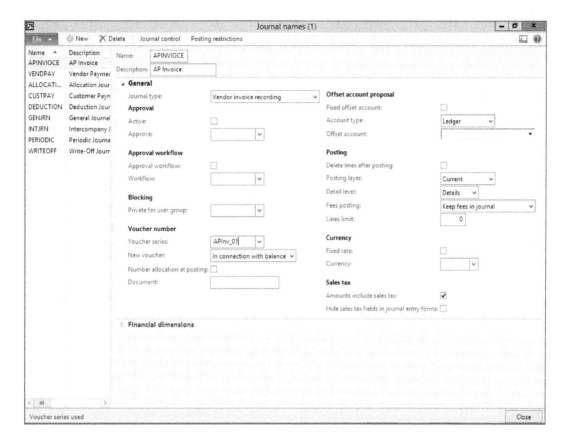

Now you will be able to select your new number sequence from the **Voucher Series** dropdown list.

Configuring Payables Journal Names

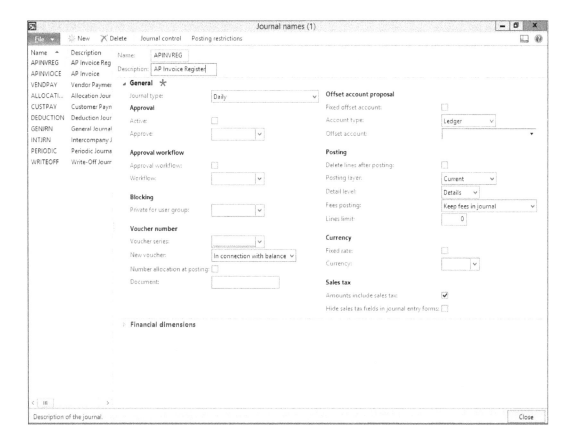

The next journal that we want to create is for the **AP Invoice Register**. To do this, click on the **New** button in the menu bar to create a new record and then set the **Name** to **APINVREG** and the **Description** to **AP Invoice Register**.

Configuring Payables Journal Names

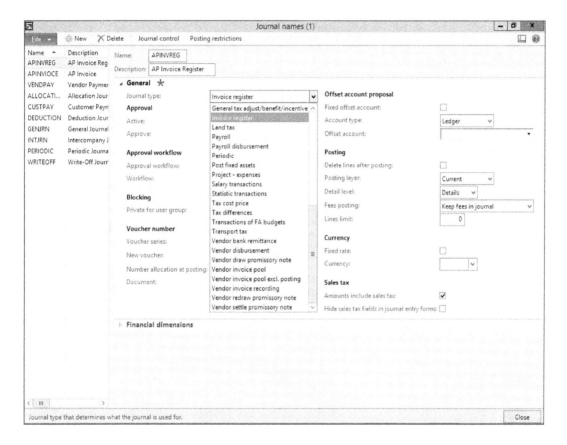

Then click on the **Journal Type** dropdown list and select the **Vendor Invoice Register** value.

Configuring Payables Journal Names

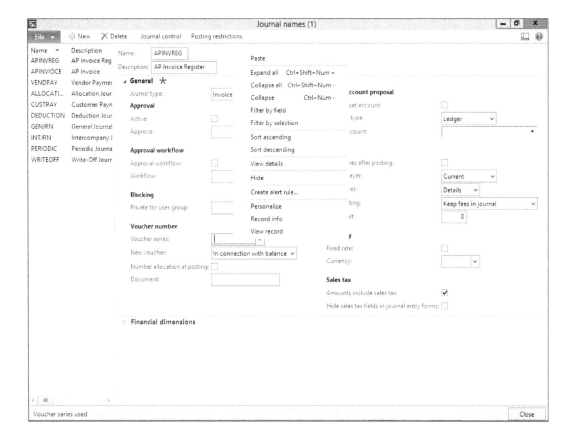

We will create a new number sequence for this journal as well by right-mouse-clicking on the **Voucher Series** field and clicking on the **View Details** menu item.

Configuring Payables Journal Names

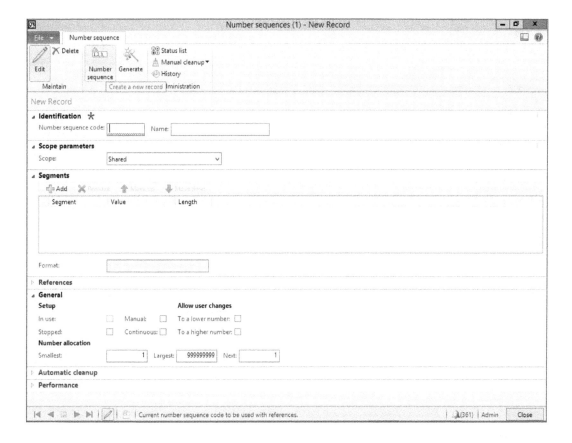

When the **Number Sequences** maintenance form is displayed, click on the **Number Sequence** button within the **New** group of the **Number Sequence** ribbon bar to create a new record.

Configuring Payables Journal Names

Set the **Number Sequence Code** to **APInvReg01** and the **Name** to **AP Invoice Register**.

Configuring Payables Journal Names

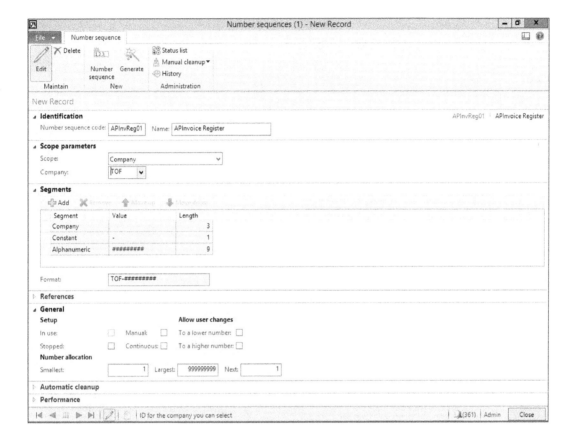

Change the **Scope** to **Company** and then click on the **Company** dropdown list and select the company that you want to assign the number sequence to.

Configuring Payables Journal Names

Then change the **Constant** value within the **Segments** table to **–APIR-** to uniquely identify your AP Invoice Journal journals.

Configuring Payables Journal Names

Finally, check the **Continuous** flag within the **General** tab group.

Then click on the **Close** button to exit from the form.

Configuring Payables Journal Names

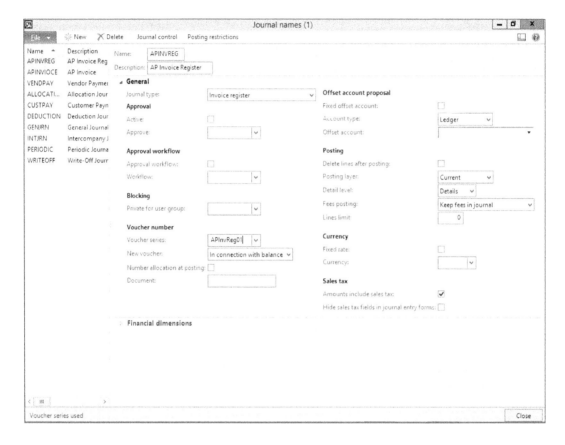

Now you will be able to select your new number sequence from the **Voucher Series** dropdown list.

Configuring Payables Journal Names

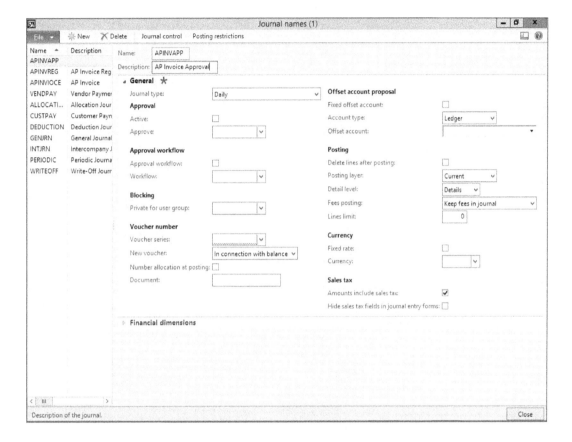

The final journal that we want to create is for the **AP Invoice Approvals**. To do this, click on the **New** button in the menu bar to create a new record and then set the **Name** to **APINVAPP** and the **Description** to **AP Invoice Approval**.

Configuring Payables Journal Names

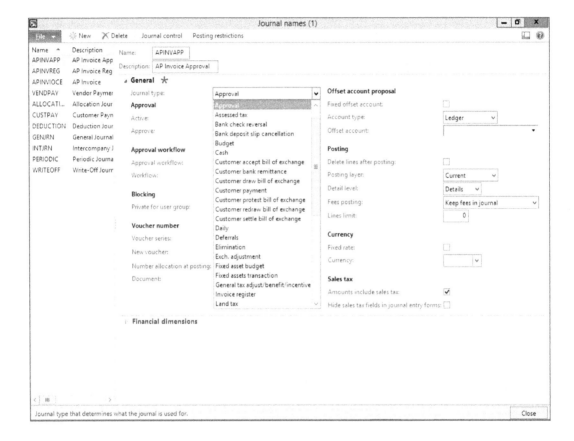

Then click on the **Journal Type** dropdown list and select the **Approval** value.

Configuring Payables Journal Names

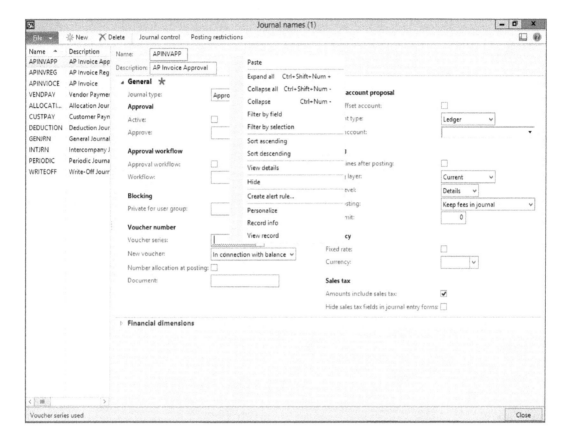

We will create a new number sequence for this journal as well by right-mouse-clicking on the **Voucher Series** field and clicking on the **View Details** menu item.

Configuring Payables Journal Names

When the **Number Sequences** maintenance form is displayed, click on the **Number Sequence** button within the **New** group of the **Number Sequence** ribbon bar to create a new record.

Configuring Payables Journal Names

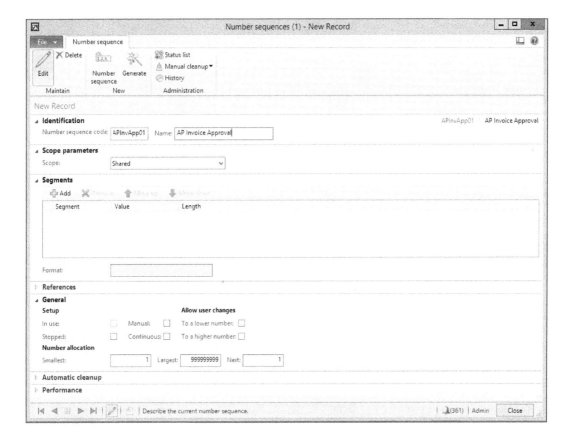

Set the **Number Sequence Code** to **APInvApp01** and the **Name** to **AP Invoice Approval**.

Configuring Payables Journal Names

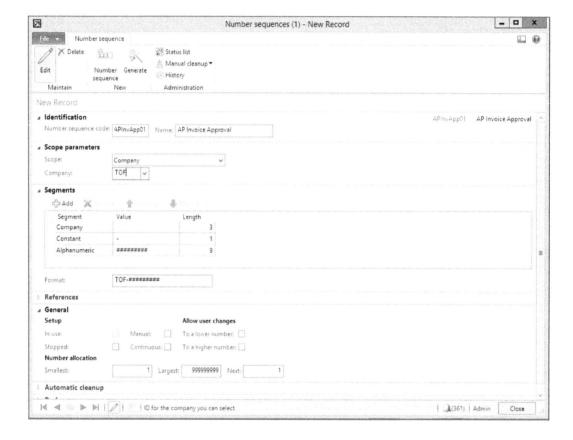

Change the **Scope** to **Company** and then click on the **Company** dropdown list and select the company that you want to assign the number sequence to.

Configuring Payables Journal Names

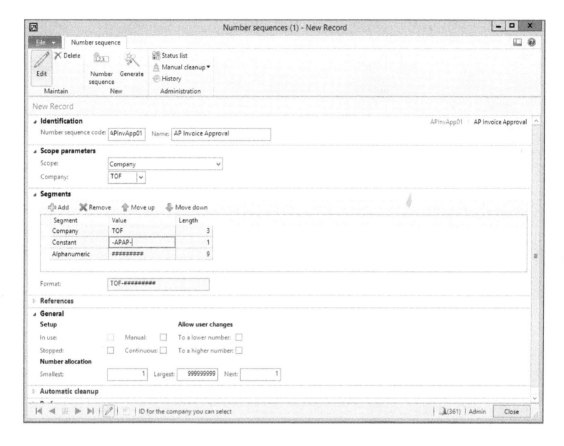

Then change the **Constant** value within the **Segments** table to **–APAP-** to uniquely identify your AP Invoice Journal journals.

Configuring Payables Journal Names

Finally, check the **Continuous** flag within the **General** tab group.

Then click on the **Close** button to exit from the form.

Configuring Payables Journal Names

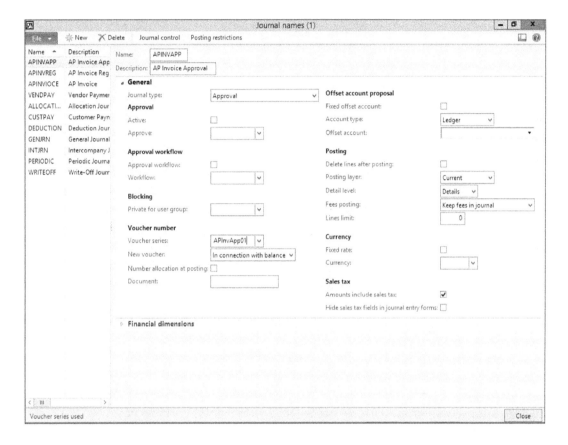

Now you will be able to select your new number sequence from the **Voucher Series** dropdown list.

Now that you have all of the journals created, just click on the **Close** button to exit from the form.

Configuring Vendor Posting Profiles

The next setup task that we will need to perform is to configure a set of default Posting Profiles for the Payables area. These are used to default in common posting accounts and configurations for all, or groups of vendors. We will want to create two of these profiles initially, one for our General postings, and another for Pre-payments.

Configuring Vendor Posting Profiles

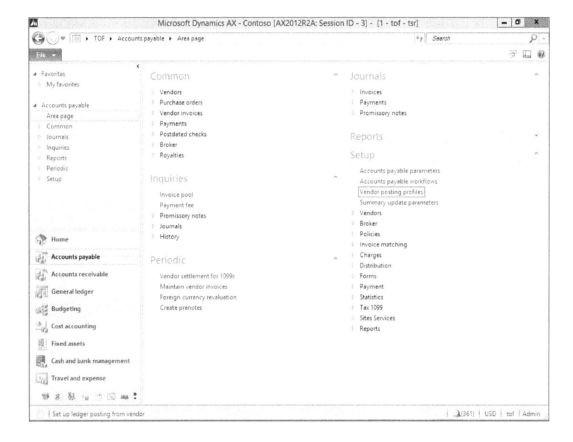

To do this, click on the **Vendor Posting Profiles** menu item within the **Setup** group of the **Accounts Payable** area page.

Configuring Vendor Posting Profiles

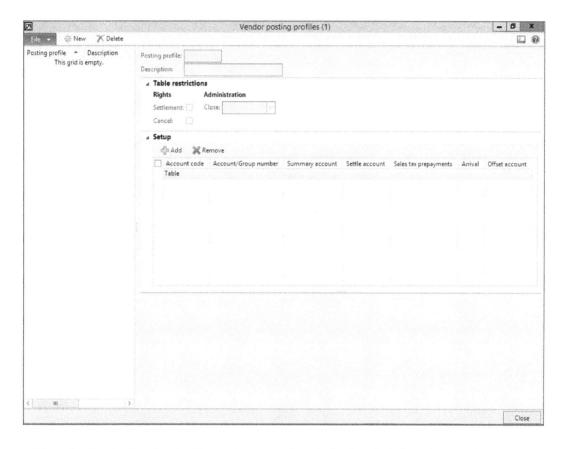

When the **Vendor Posting Profiles** maintenance form is displayed, click on the **New** button in the menu bar to create a new record.

Configuring Vendor Posting Profiles

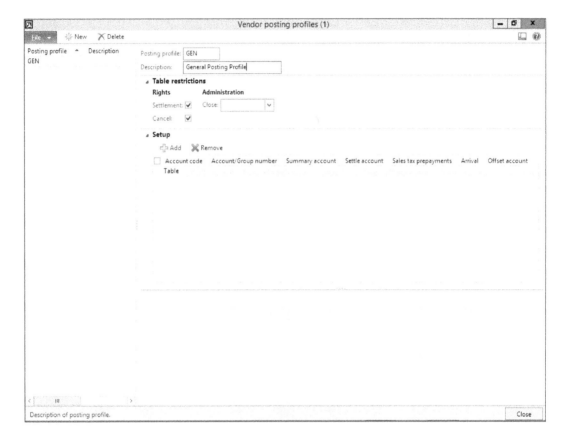

Then set the **Posting Profile** to **GEN** and the **Description** to **General Posting Profile**.

Configuring Vendor Posting Profiles

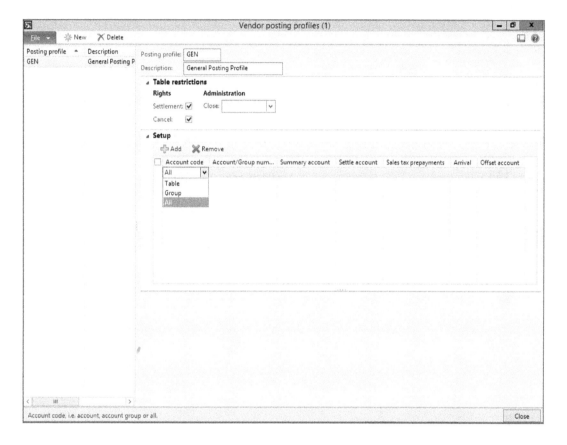

Within the **Setup** tab group, click on the **Add** button to create a new record and then set the **Account Code** field to **All** to create a posting profile that will apply to all of the vendors.

Configuring Vendor Posting Profiles

Click on the **Summary Account** dropdown list and select the main account that you want to post to – we will use **211100**.

Configuring Vendor Posting Profiles

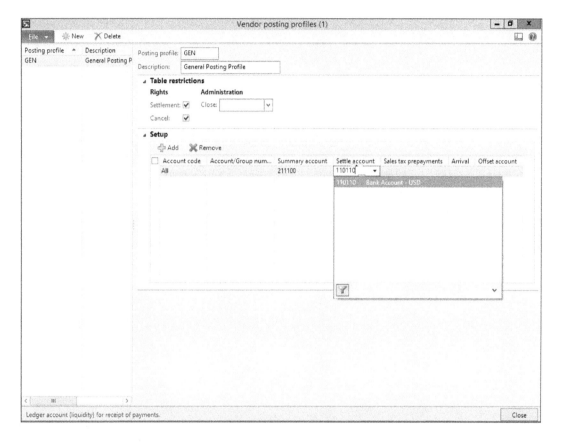

Then click on the **Settle Account** dropdown list and select the account that you want to post the settled amounts to – in this example we use the bank account which is **110110**.

Configuring Vendor Posting Profiles

Then select the main account for the **Arrival** field – we will use **211310**.

Configuring Vendor Posting Profiles

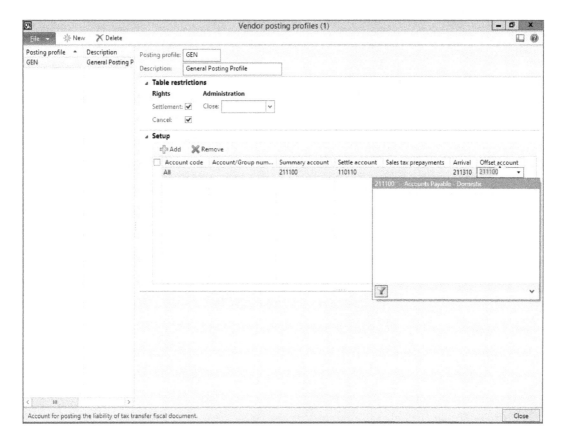

Finally, click on the dropdown list for the **Offset Account** and select the main account that you want to post the payables to – we will use **211100**.

Configuring Vendor Posting Profiles

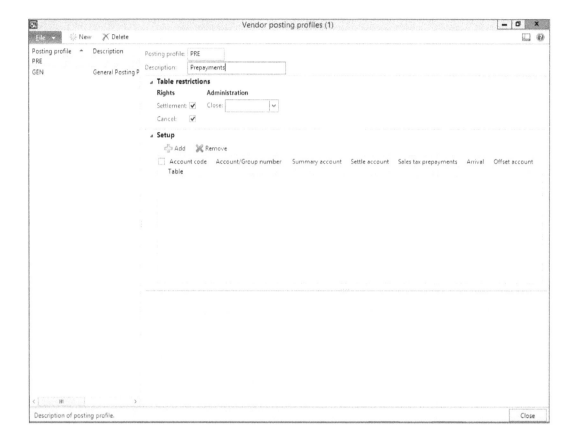

Next we will create a posting profile for prepayments. To do this, click on the **New** button in the menu bar to create a new record and then set the **Posting Profile** code to **PRE** and the **Description** to **Prepayments**.

Configuring Vendor Posting Profiles

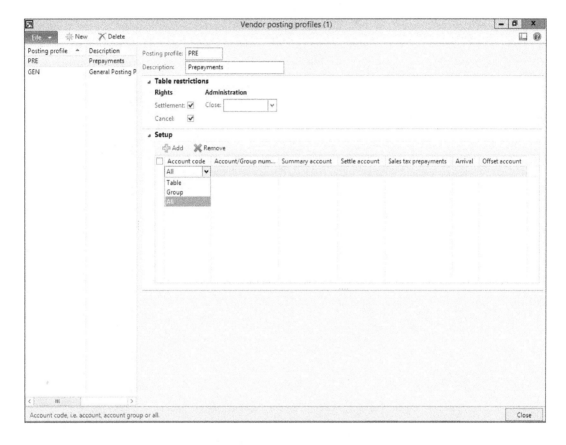

Within the **Setup** tab group, click on the **Add** button to create a new record and then set the **Account Code** field to **All** to create a posting profile that will apply to all of the vendors.

Configuring Vendor Posting Profiles

Click on the dropdown list for the **Summary Account** and select the main account that you want to post your summary prepayments to – we will use **211100**.

Then click on the dropdown list for the **Settle Account** and select the main account that you want to post your settlements to – we will use the bank account **110110**.

And then, click on the dropdown list for the **Sales Tax Prepayments** and select the main account that you want to post your sales tax prepayments to – we will use **221850**.

Configuring Vendor Posting Profiles

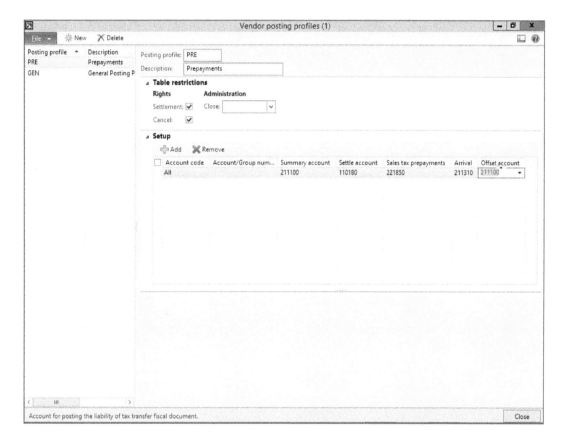

Finally, click on the dropdown list for the **Offset Account** and select the main account that you want to post the payables to – we will use **211100**.

After you have done that you are finished with the Vendor Posting Profiles and you can click on the **Close** button to exit from the form.

Configuring Cash Payment Terms

Now we can start configuring some of the codes and controls to manage your cash payments. We will start with this is to configure your **Cash Payment Terms** so that you can assign them to your vendor accounts later on.

Configuring Cash Payment Terms

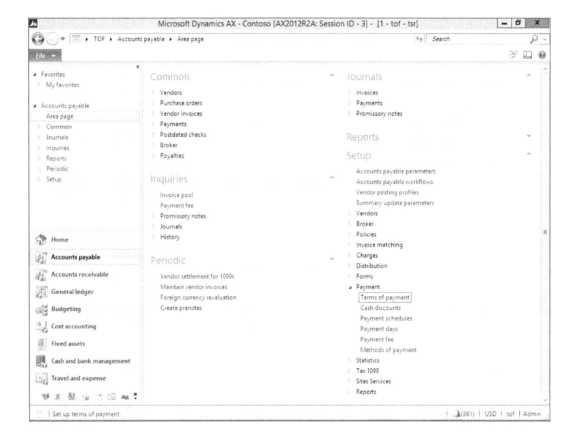

To do this click on the **Terms Of Payment** menu item within the **Payment** folder of the **Setup** group within the **Accounts Payable** area page.

Configuring Cash Payment Terms

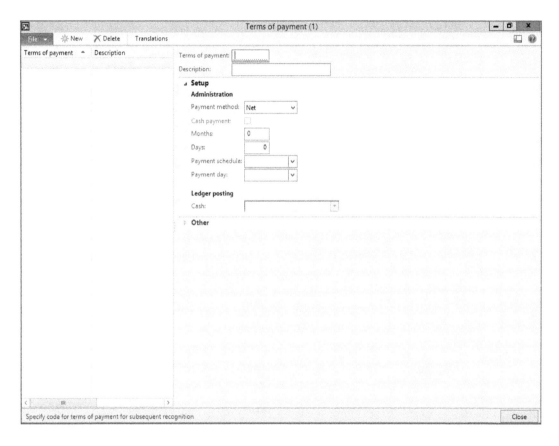

When the **Terms of Payment** maintenance form is displayed, click on the **New** button in the menu bar to create a new record.

Configuring Cash Payment Terms

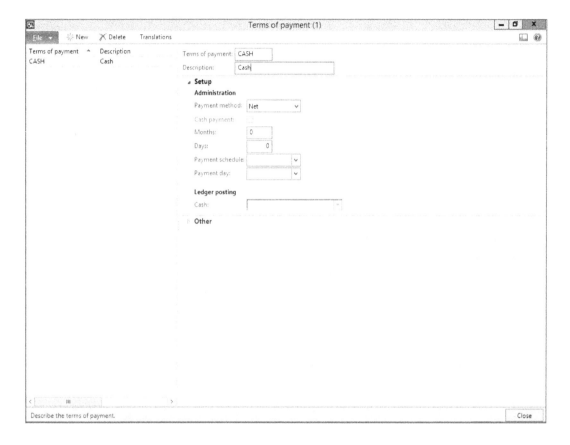

First we will create a **Cash** payment term. To do this, set the **Terms of Payment** to **CASH** and set the **Description** to **Cash**.

Configuring Cash Payment Terms

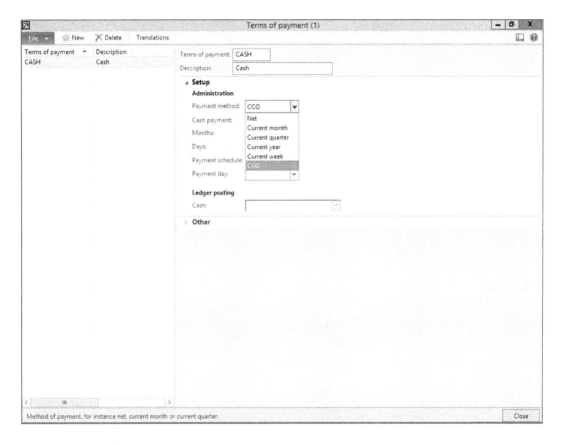

From the **Payment Method** dropdown list, select the **COD** option.

Configuring Cash Payment Terms

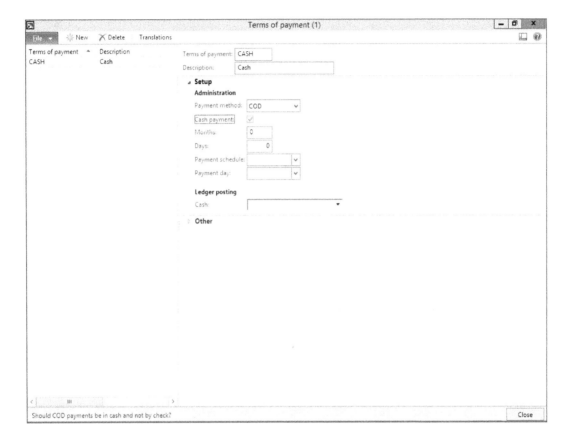

Then check the **Cash Payment** option flag.

Configuring Cash Payment Terms

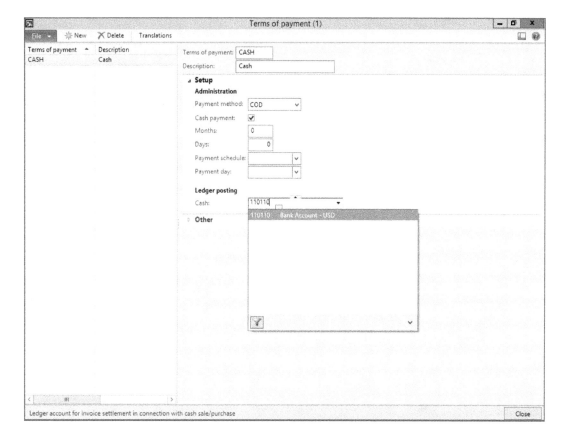

Finally, within the **Ledger Posting** field group, select the main account that you want to post to from the **Cash** field dropdown list.

Configuring Cash Payment Terms

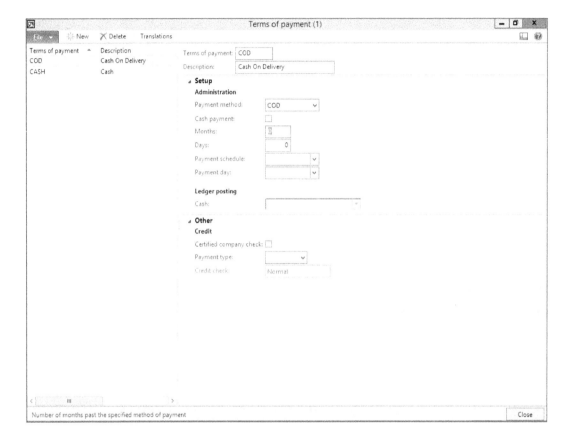

You can also create a **Cash On Delivery** Terms of Payment as well. The only difference with this record is that you do not need to check the **Cash Payment** flag.

When you are done, you can click on the **Close** button to exit from the form.

Configuring Net Days Payment Terms

Another type of Payment Term that you may want to configure is a **Net Days Payment** to pay on or before the date.

Configuring Net Days Payment Terms

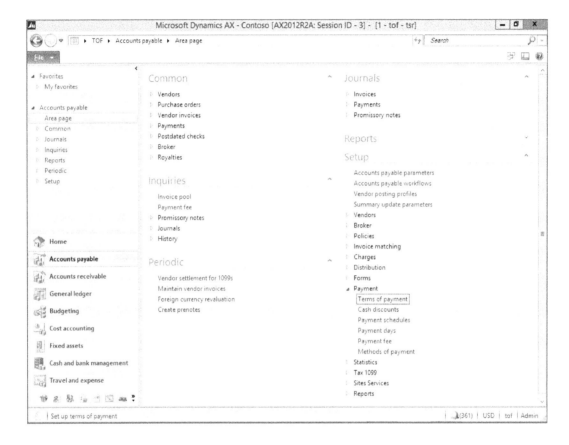

To do this click on the **Terms Of Payment** menu item within the **Payment** folder of the **Setup** group within the **Accounts Payable** area page.

Configuring Net Days Payment Terms

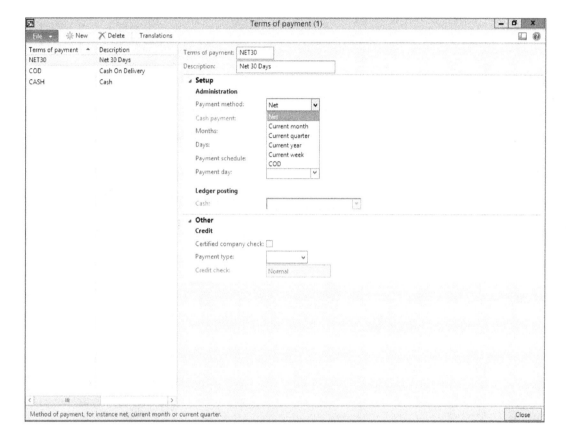

When the **Terms of Payment** maintenance form is displayed, click on the **New** button in the menu bar to create a new record.

Set your **Terms Of Payment Code** to **NET30**, and set the **Description** to **Net 30 Days**.

Then from the **Payment Method** dropdown list, select the **Net** option.

Configuring Net Days Payment Terms

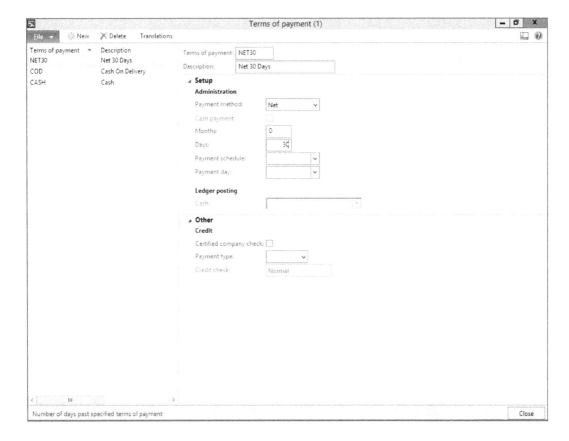

Within the **Days** field, set the number of days to **30**.

Configuring Net Days Payment Terms

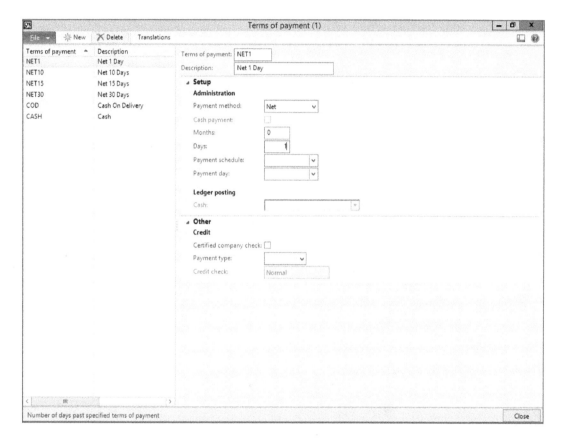

You can continue adding additional variations of the Net Payment Terms until you have all of the different options for your vendors, and then click the **Close** button to exit from the form.

Configuring Net Day Of Month Payment Terms

Another type of Payment Term that you may want to offer to your vendors is the option to pay on a certain day of the month. This requires a little additional configuration, but is still not a big deal.

Configuring Net Day Of Month Payment Terms

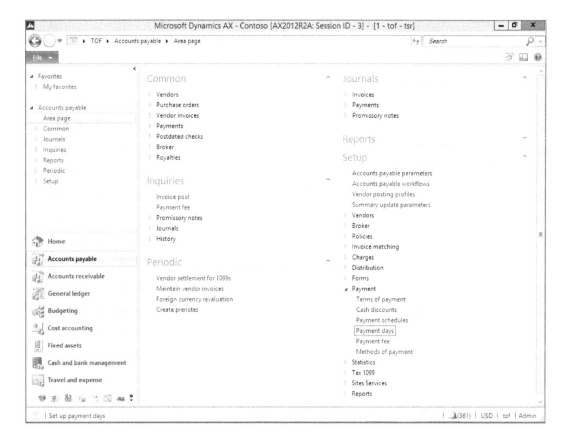

For this type of Payment Term you first need to configure the days that you want to allow. To do this, click on the **Payment Days** menu item within the **Payment** folder of the **Setup** group within the **Accounts Payable** area page.

Configuring Net Day Of Month Payment Terms

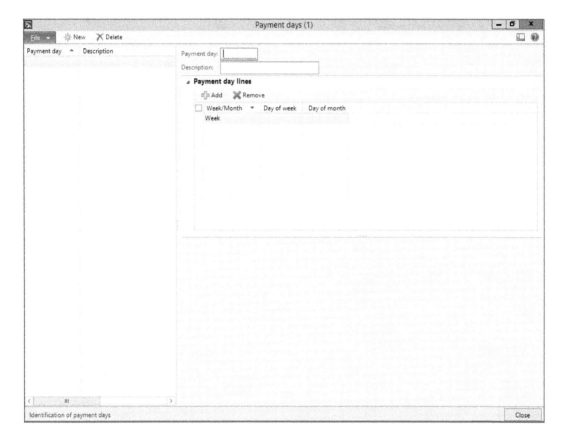

When the **Payment Days** maintenance form is displayed, click on the **New** button to add a new record.

Configuring Net Day Of Month Payment Terms

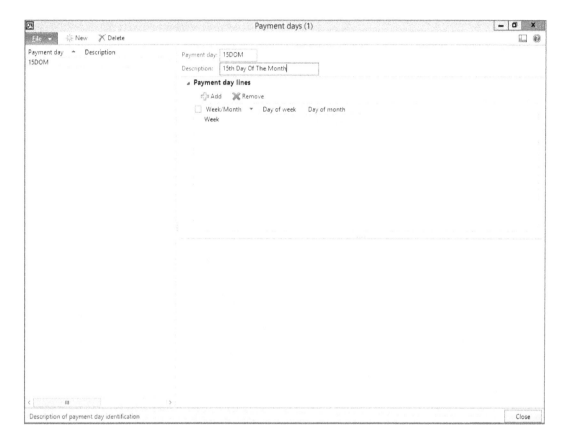

Set the **Payment Day** field to **15DOM**, and the **Description** to **15th Day Of The Month** to start defining mid-month payment terms.

Configuring Net Day Of Month Payment Terms

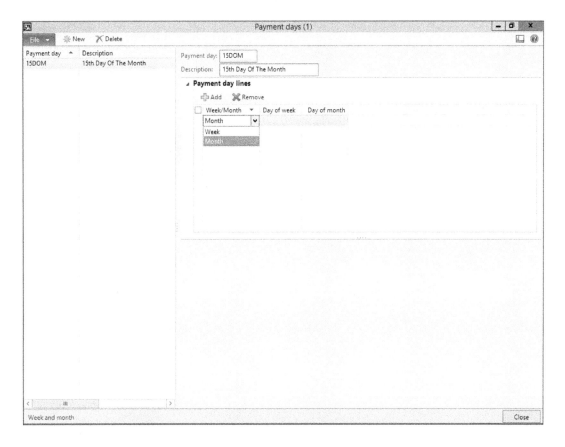

Then within the **Payment Day Lines** table, select the **Month** option from the **Week/Month** dropdown list.

Configuring Net Day Of Month Payment Terms

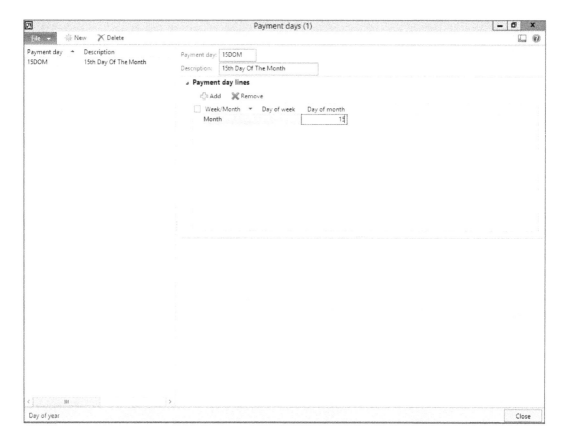

Then set the **Day Of Month** to the date that you want the payments due on, which in this case is **15**.

Configuring Net Day Of Month Payment Terms

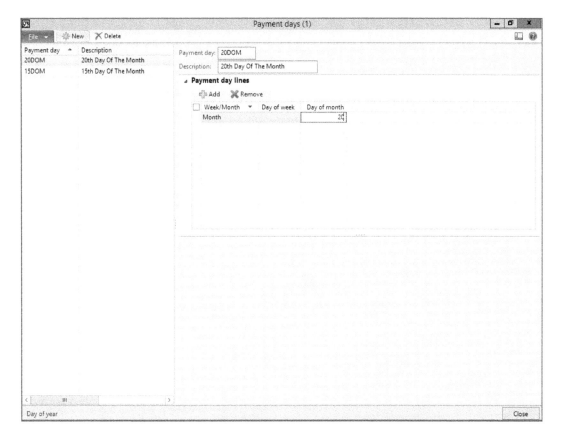

If you want to create variations of this then you can keep on adding new records.

When you are done, just click the **Close** button to exit from the form.

Configuring Net Day Of Month Payment Terms

Now return to the **Terms Of Payment** maintenance form, and click on the **New** button to add a new record.

Set the **Terms Of Payment** to **DOM15**, and the **Description** to **15th Day Of The Month**.

Configuring Net Day Of Month Payment Terms

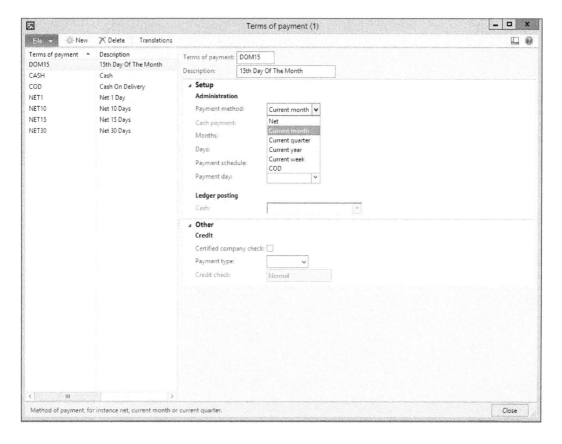

From the **Payment Method** dropdown, select the **Current Month** option.

Configuring Net Day Of Month Payment Terms

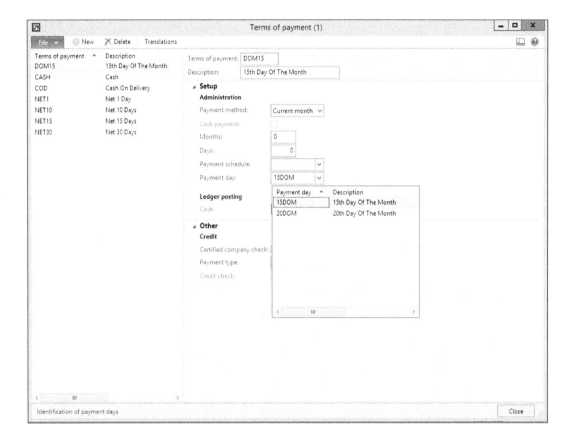

And then from the **Payment Day** dropdown field select the **15DOM** record that you just created.

Configuring Net Day Of Month Payment Terms

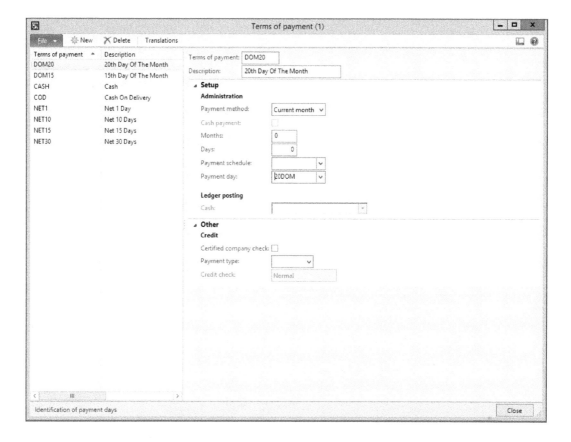

If you created any additional Payment Day records, then you can repeat the process to add additional **Terms Of Payment** for them.

Configuring Equal Monthly Scheduled Payment Terms

Payment terms don't have to be just a lump sum payment, you can also configure payment schedules with multiple payment dates. The first type of payment schedule that you may want to configure is a monthly payment for a set number of months.

Configuring Equal Monthly Scheduled Payment Terms

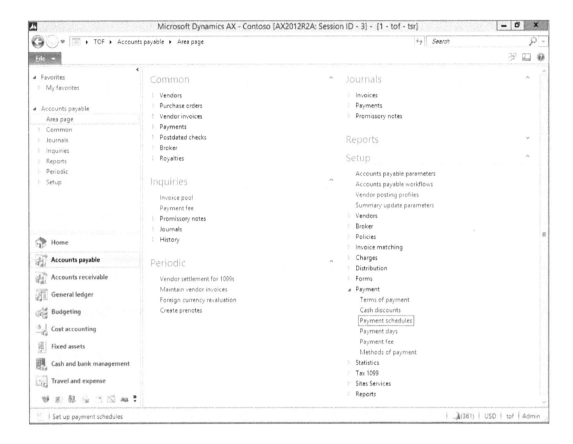

To do this, click on the **Payment Schedules** menu item within the **Payment** folder of the **Setup** group within the **Accounts Payable** area page.

Configuring Equal Monthly Scheduled Payment Terms

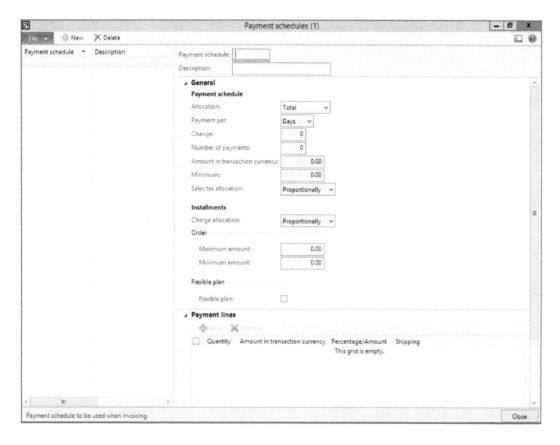

When the **Payment Schedules** maintenance form is displayed, click on the **New** button in the menu bar to create a new record.

Configuring Equal Monthly Scheduled Payment Terms

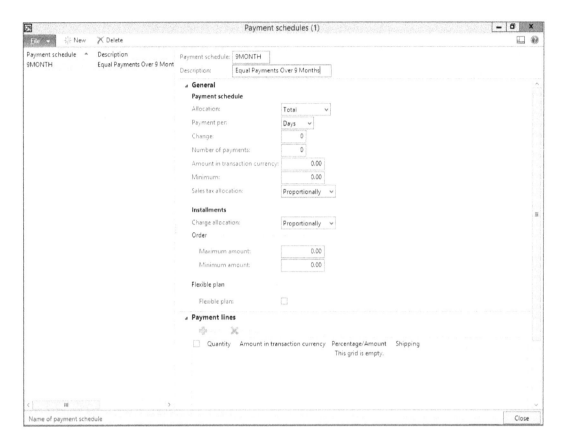

Then set the **Payment Schedule** code to **9MONTH** and the description to **Equal Payments Over 9 Months**.

Configuring Equal Monthly Scheduled Payment Terms

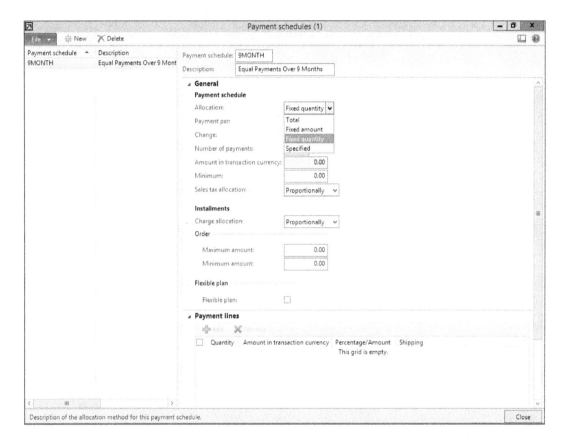

From the **Allocation** field drop down, select the **Fixed Quantity** option to tell the system that you want to have equal payments over a set number of intervals.

Configuring Equal Monthly Scheduled Payment Terms

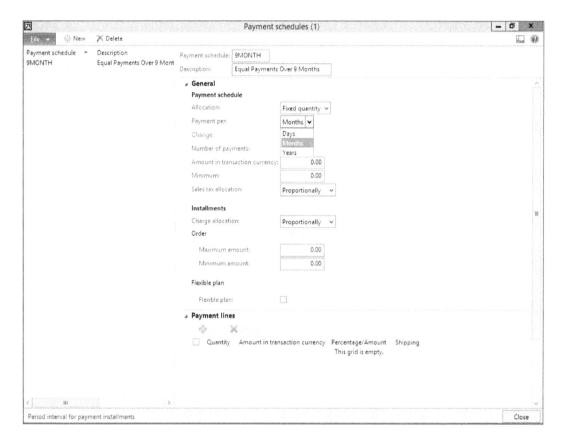

Then select the **Months** option from the **Payment Per** dropdown list.

Configuring Equal Monthly Scheduled Payment Terms

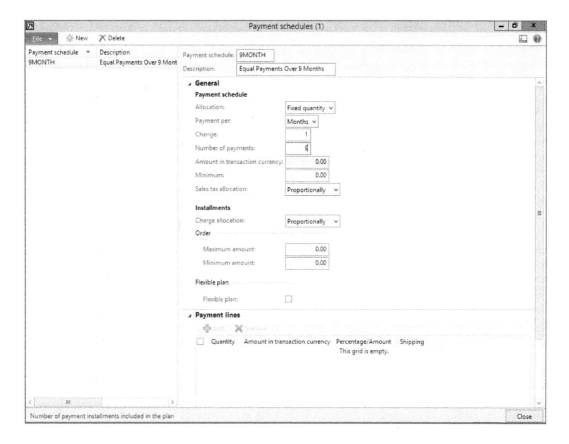

Then type in the **Number Of Payments** that you want to have within the schedule. In this case we chose **9**.

After you have done this you can add additional payment schedule variations, and when you are done, just click on the **Close** button to exit from the form.

Configuring Equal Monthly Scheduled Payment Terms

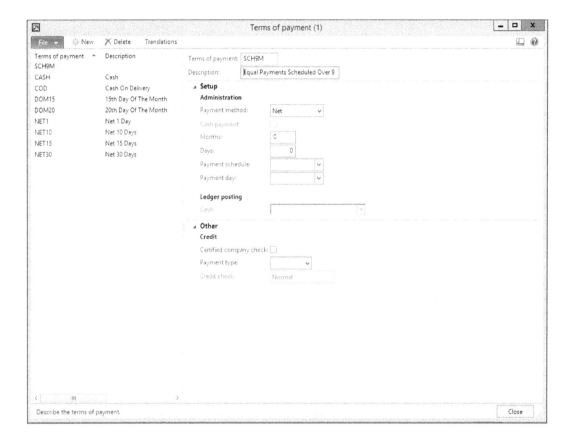

Now return to the **Terms Of Payments** maintenance form and click the **New** button in the menu bar to create a new record.

Then set the **Terms Of Payment** code to be **SCH6M** and the **Description** to **Equal Payments Scheduled over 9 Months**.

Configuring Equal Monthly Scheduled Payment Terms

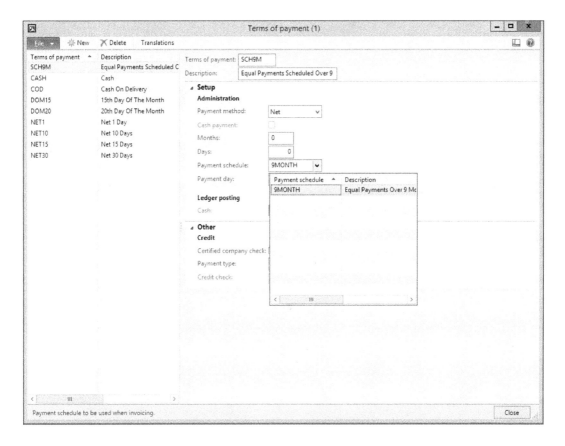

Set the **Payment Method** to be **Net** and then from the **Payment Schedule** field, select the new monthly schedule that you just created.

After you have done that you can click on the **Close** button and exit from the form.

Configuring Proportional Monthly Scheduled Payment Terms

Another variation of the monthly payment schedule that you can create within Dynamics AX is a proportional payment schedule with varying payment percentages by month. With this you could required lump sums up front, or have balloon payments structured at the end of the payments.

Configuring Proportional Monthly Scheduled Payment Terms

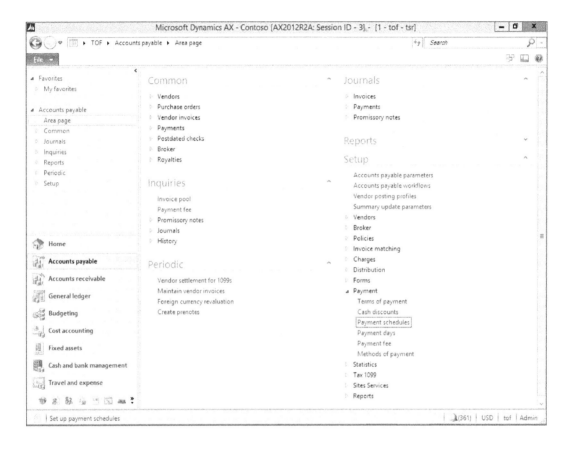

To do this, click on the **Payment Schedules** menu item within the **Payment** folder of the **Setup** group within the **Accounts Payable** area page.

Configuring Proportional Monthly Scheduled Payment Terms

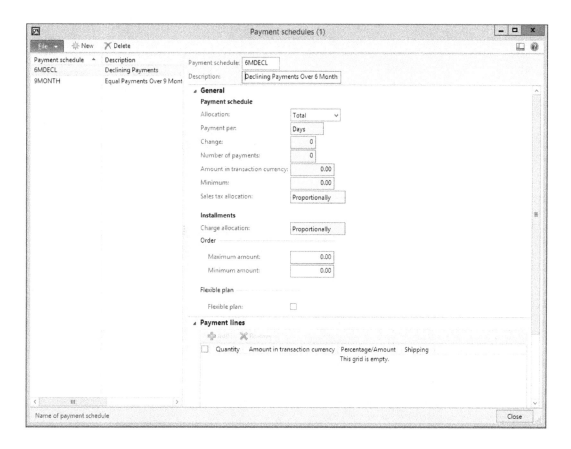

When the **Payment Schedules** maintenance form is displayed, click on the **New** button in the menu bar to create a new record.

Then set the **Payment Schedule** code to **6MDECL** and the description to **Declining Payments Over 6 Months**.

Configuring Proportional Monthly Scheduled Payment Terms

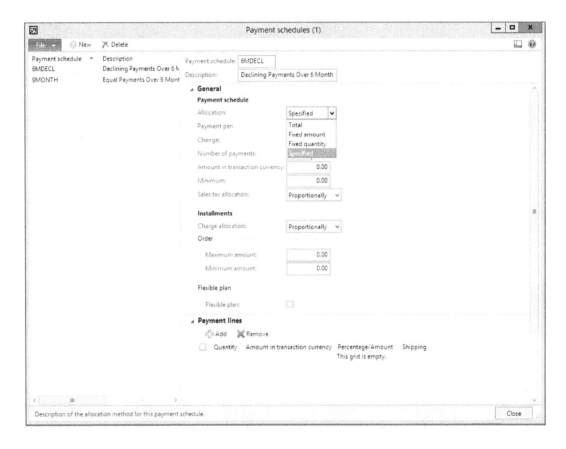

Then from the **Allocation** dropdown list select the **Specified** option.

Configuring Proportional Monthly Scheduled Payment Terms

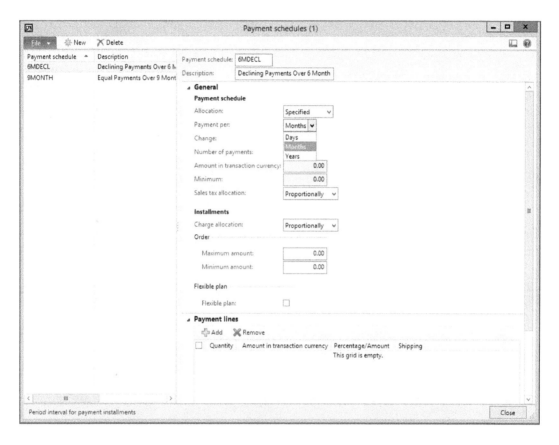

Set the **Payment Term** field to **Months** to identify that we are going to have monthly payments.

Configuring Proportional Monthly Scheduled Payment Terms

Now collapse the **General group** so that you can see the **Payment Lines** tab group.

Configuring Proportional Monthly Scheduled Payment Terms

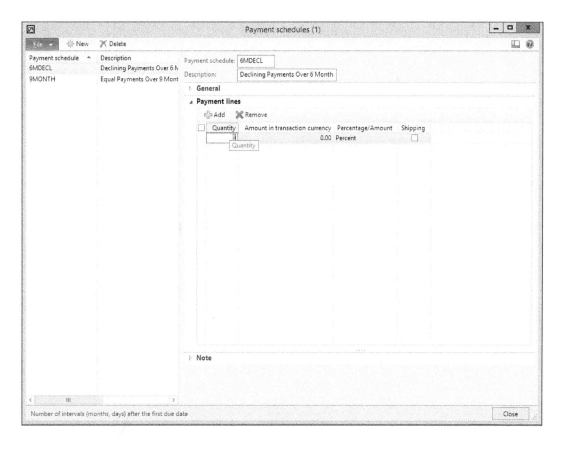

Click on the **Add** button in the **Payment Lines** table to create a new payment line record and set the **Quantity** to 1 to create a record for the first month.

Configuring Proportional Monthly Scheduled Payment Terms

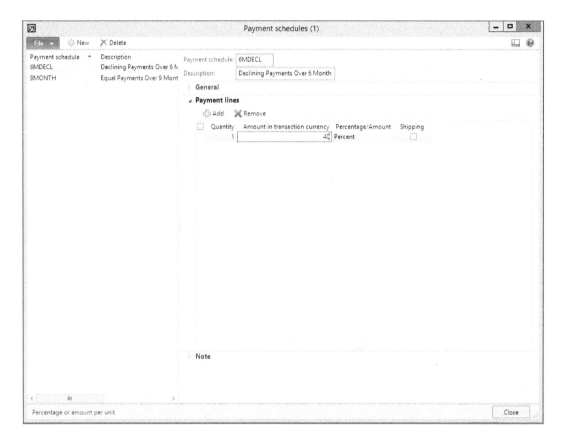

Then set the **Amount In Transaction Currency** field to be the percentage of payment that is due in that first month.

Configuring Proportional Monthly Scheduled Payment Terms

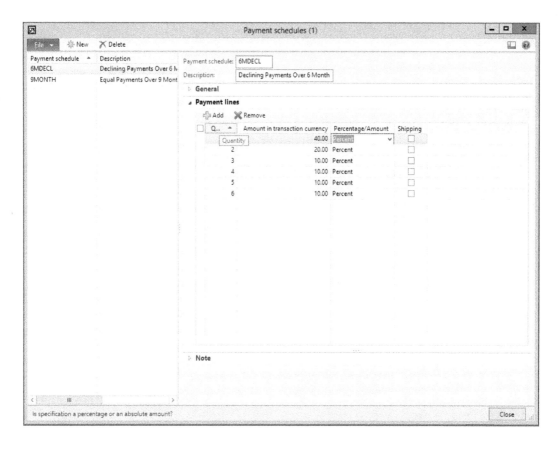

Repeat the process for all of the other months that you require payments along with the percentage amount. Make sure that they add up to 100% so that you are not giving away money.

When you are done, click on the **Close** button to exit from the form.

Configuring Proportional Monthly Scheduled Payment Terms

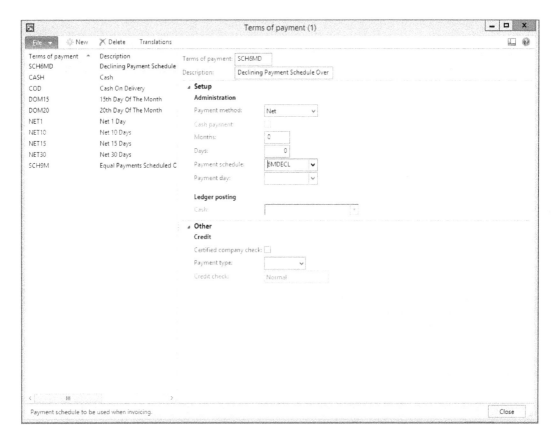

Now return to the **Terms Of Payments** maintenance form and click the **New** button in the menu bar to create a new record.

Then set the **Terms Of Payment** code to be **SCH6M** and the **Description** to **Equal Payments Scheduled over 9 Months**.

Set the **Payment Method** to be **Net** and then from the **Payment Schedule** field, select the new proportional monthly schedule that you just created.

After you have done that you can click on the **Close** button and exit from the form.

Configuring Cash Discount Codes

In addition to configuring the **Terms Of Payments** you may also want to configure **Cash Discount Codes** as incentives for early payment with discount percentages.

Configuring Cash Discount Codes

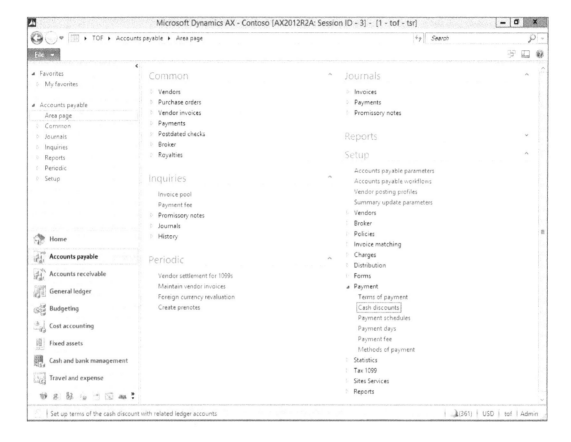

To do this, click on the **Cash Discounts** menu item within the **Payments** folder of the **Setup** group of the **Accounts Payable** area page.

Configuring Cash Discount Codes

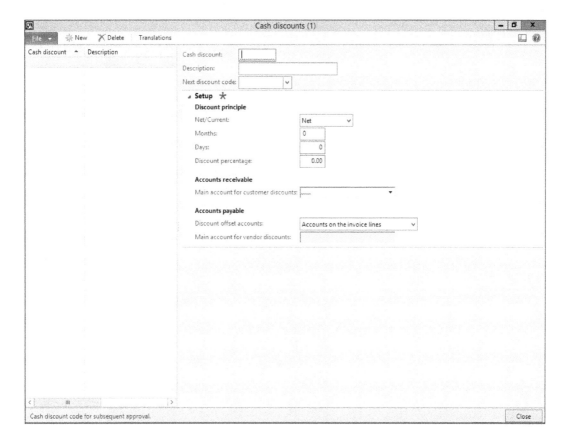

When the **Cash Discounts** maintenance form is displayed, click on the **New** button in the menu bar to create a new record.

Configuring Cash Discount Codes

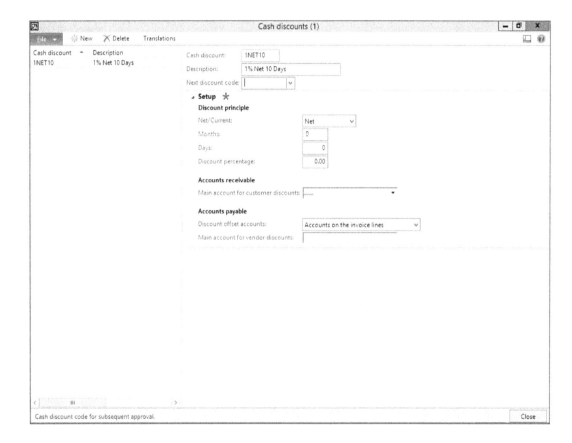

Then set the **Cash Discount** code to **1NET10** and the **Description** to **1% Net 10** which seems like a reasonable discount to give for early payment.

Configuring Cash Discount Codes

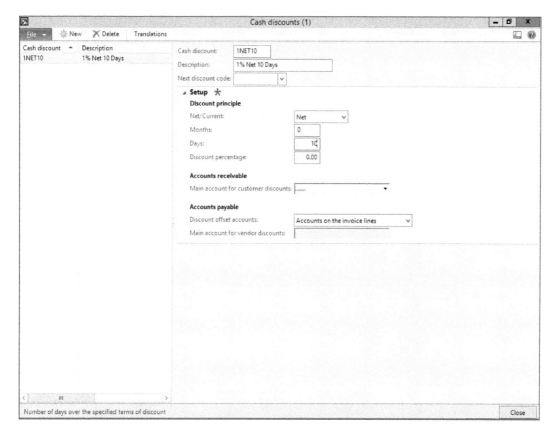

Set the **Days** field to be the number of days that your vendor wants to encourage you to pay in – in our case **10**.

Configuring Cash Discount Codes

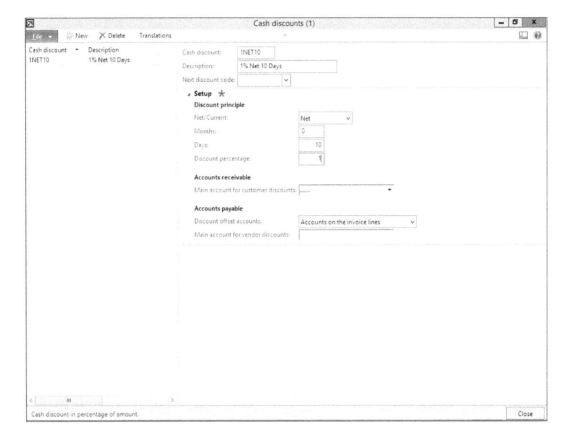

And then in the **Discount Percentage** field set the discount percentage that you are being given by your vendor. We set ours to **1**.

Configuring Cash Discount Codes

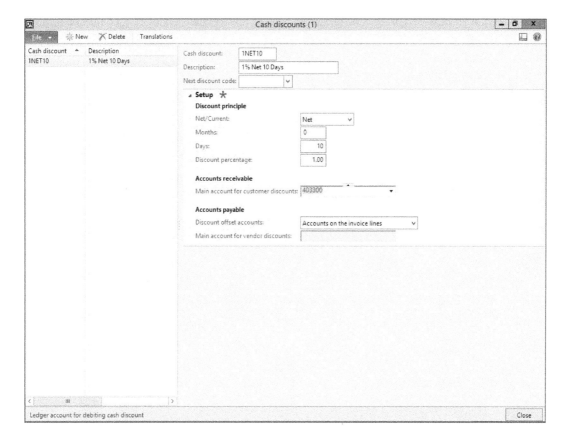

These Cash Discounts codes are also used for the Accounts Receivable discounts – no point in reinventing the wheel. So while we are here we will also configure the AR settings for the discounts so that we don't need to set them up later on. To do this assign a **Main Account For Customer Discounts** to identify where the discount is going to be posted to.

Configuring Cash Discount Codes

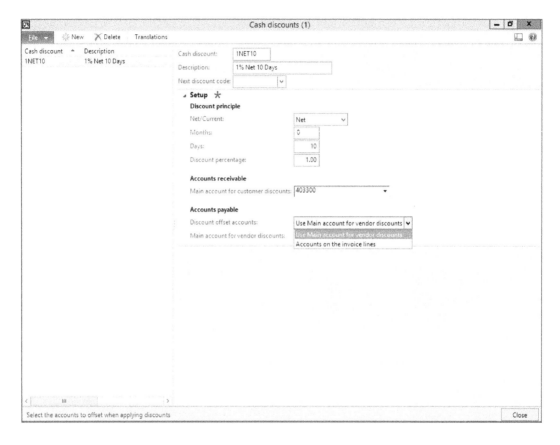

Then select the **Use Main Account For Vendor Discounts** option from the **Discount Offset Accounts** field.

Configuring Cash Discount Codes

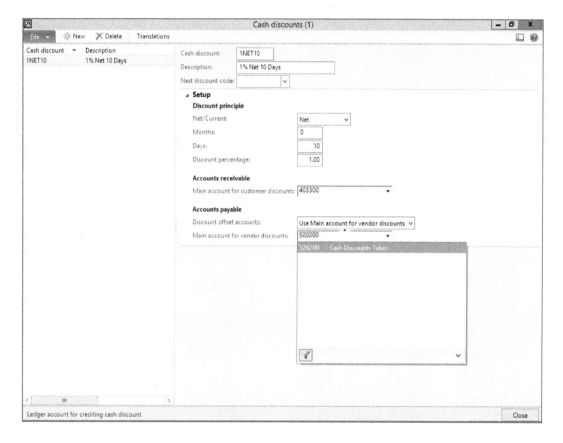

And then select the **Main Account For Vendor Discounts** that you want to post the Vendor Discounts to.

Configuring Cash Discount Codes

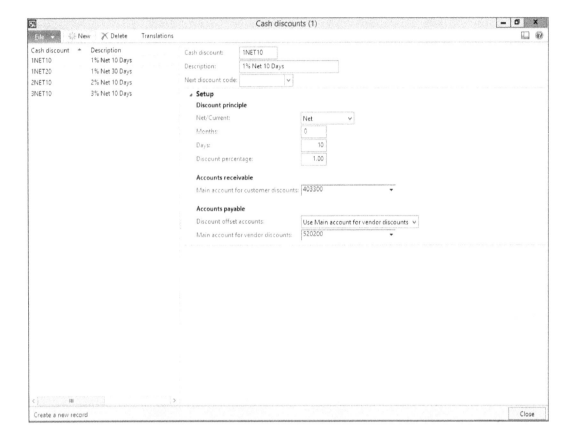

You can repeat this process for any other combinations and variations of the discount terms that you want to have with your vendors, and when you a done, just click on the **Close** button to exit from the form.

Configuring A Check Payment Method

Now we will want to set up the **Methods Of Payment** that you will want to allow through the system. The first one that we will start with is the **Check** method of payment.

Configuring A Check Payment Method

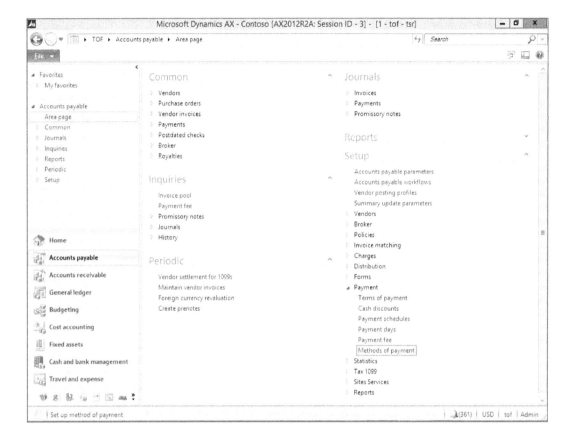

To do this, click on the **Methods of Payment** menu item within the **Payment** folder of the **Setup** group within the **Accounts Payable** area page.

Configuring A Check Payment Method

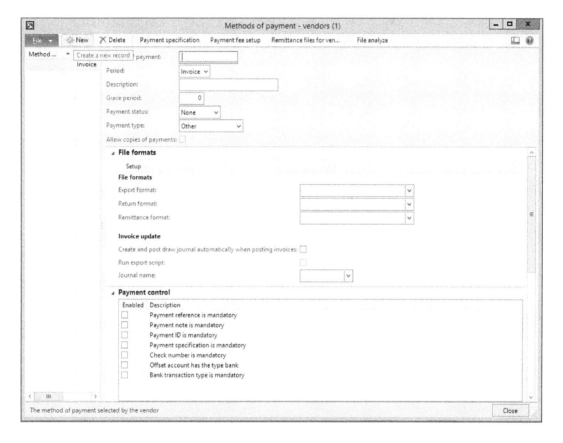

When the **Methods Of Payment** maintenance form is displayed, click on the **New** button in the menu bar to create a new record.

Configuring A Check Payment Method

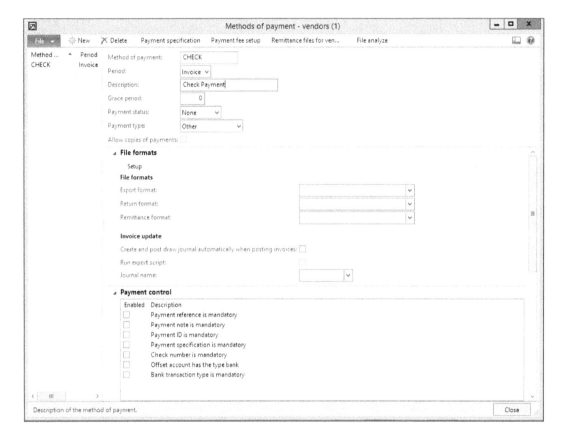

Then set the **Method Of Payment** code to **CHECK** and the **Description** to **Check Payment**.

Configuring A Check Payment Method

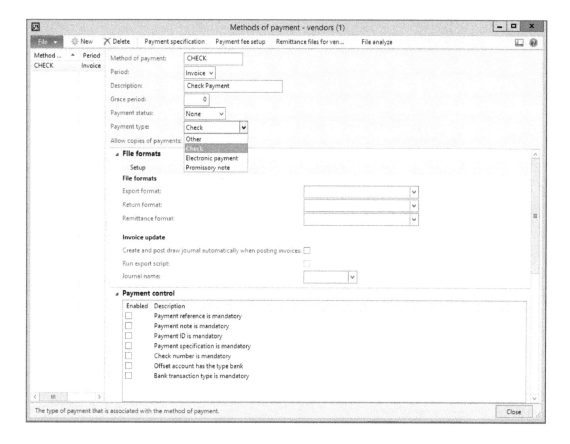

Click on the **Payment Type** dropdown list and select the **Check** option.

Configuring A Check Payment Method

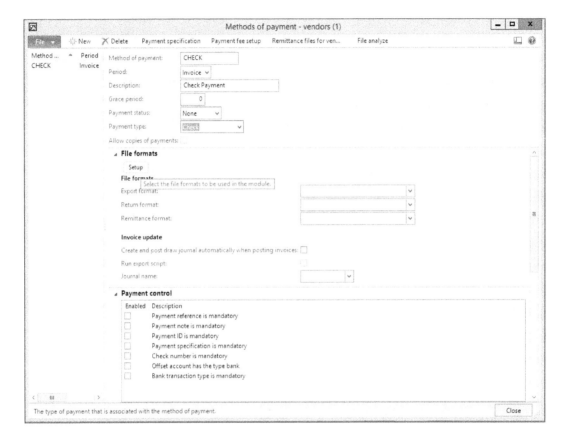

Now we need to specify our file formats for exporting the checks. To do this though we need to specify the formats within AIF that we want to use. To do this, click on the **Setup** button within the **File Formats** tab group.

Configuring A Check Payment Method

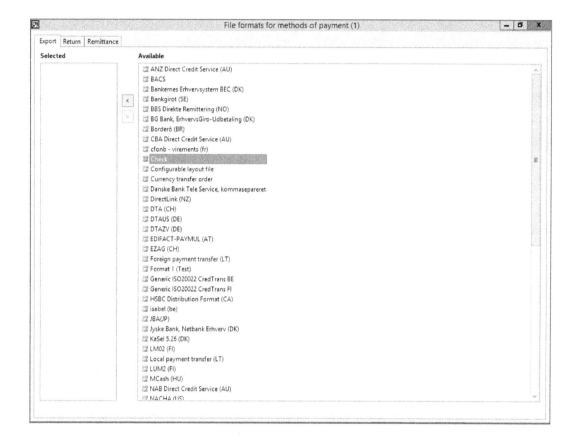

When the **File Formats For Methods Of Payment** form is displayed, find the **Check** format within the **Export** tab and then click on the **<** button.

Configuring A Check Payment Method

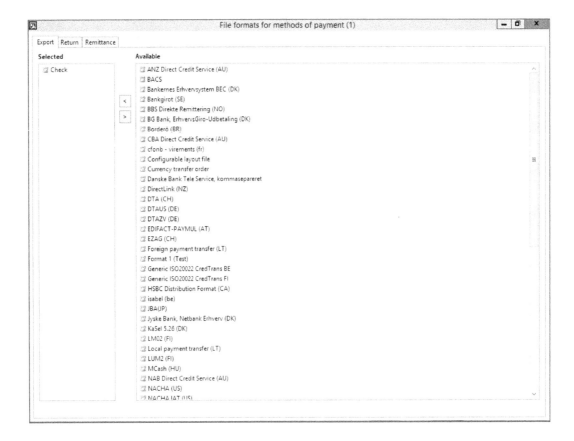

After the **Check** format has been added to the **Selected** list you can close out of the form.

Configuring A Check Payment Method

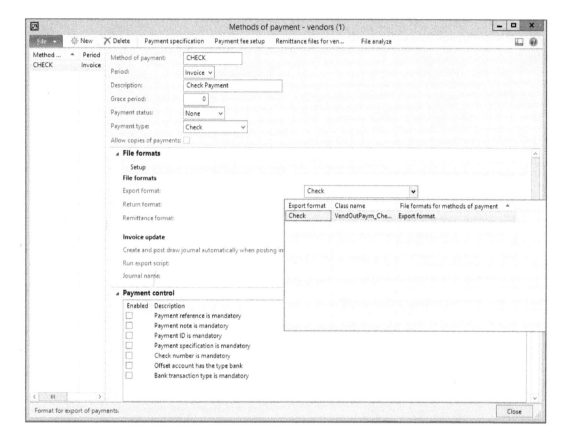

When you return back to the **Methods Of Payments** form you can click on the **Export Format** dropdown list and select the **Check** export format.

Configuring A Check Payment Method

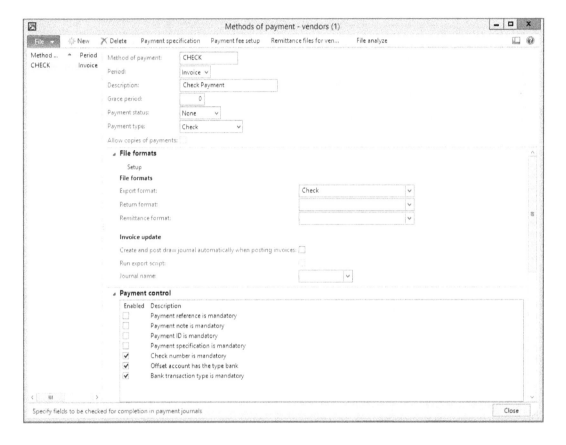

Now expand out the **Payment Control** tab group and check the **Check Number Is Mandatory**, **Offset Account Has The Type Bank**, and also the **Bank Transaction Type Is Mandatory** flags to add a little control around the check printing.

Configuring A Check Payment Method

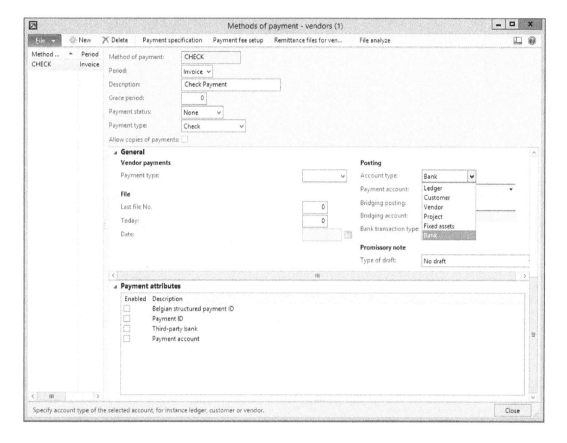

Next open up the **General** tab group, and click on the **Account Type** within the **Posting** field group, and select the **Bank** option.

Configuring A Check Payment Method

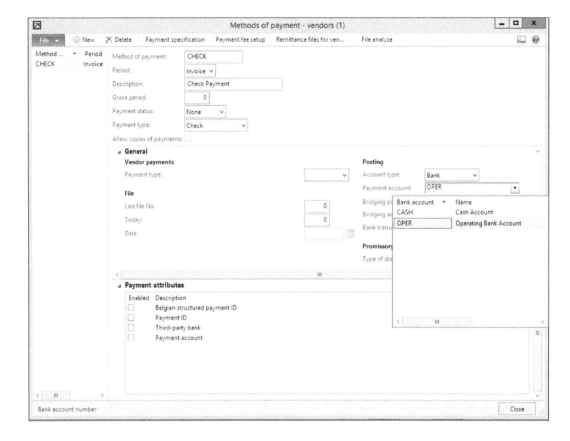

Then click on the **Payment Account** dropdown list and select the bank account that you want to use by default for the check payments.

Configuring A Check Payment Method

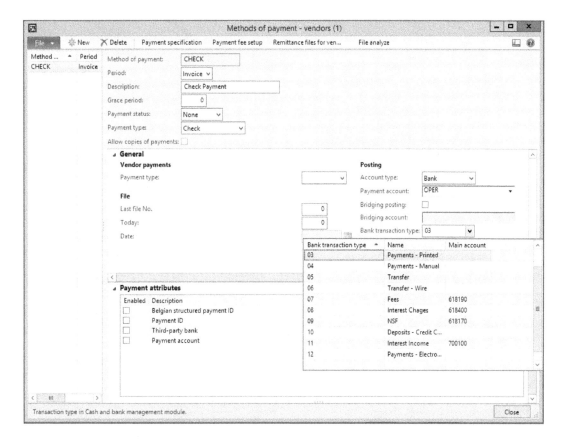

Finally, click on the **Bank Transaction Type** dropdown list and select the default transaction type for the check payments – we will use **03**.

Configuring A Check Payment Method

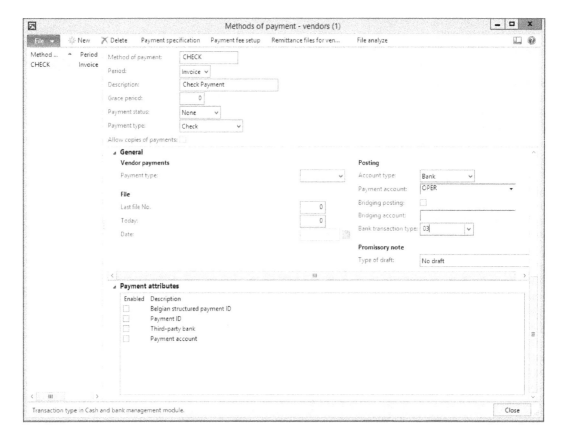

After you have done that you are done with the check payment setup.

Configuring An Electronic Payment Method

Another payment method that you may want to configure is an Electronic Payment.

Configuring An Electronic Payment Method

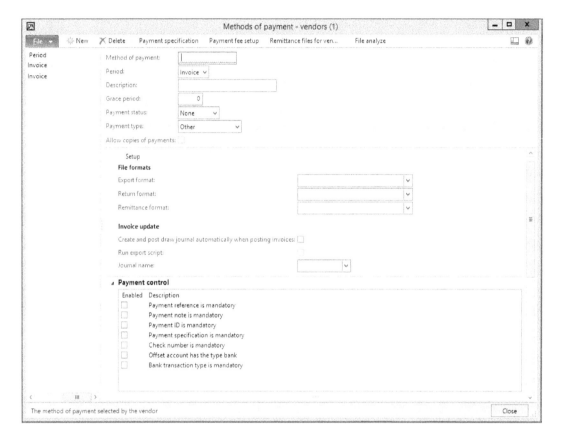

To do this return to the **Methods Of Payments** maintenance form and click on the **New** button within the menu bar to create a new record.

Configuring An Electronic Payment Method

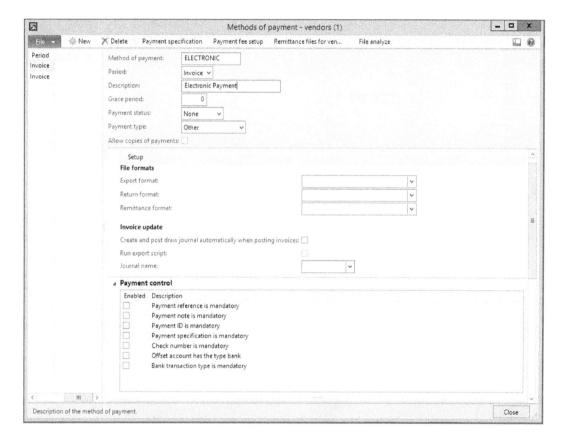

Then set the **Method of Payment** code to **ELECTRONIC** and the **Description** to **Electronic Payment**.

Configuring An Electronic Payment Method

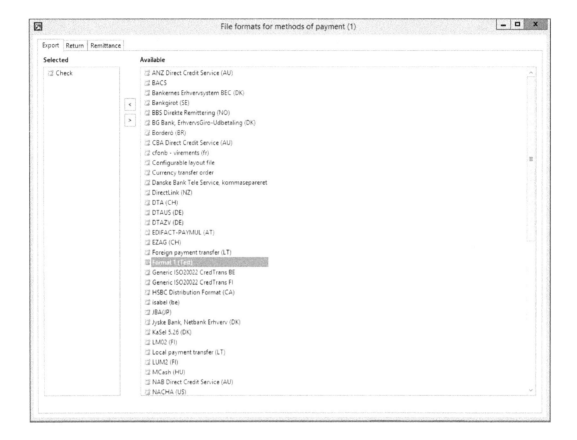

Again, we need to specify our file formats for exporting the electronic payments within AIF. To do this, click on the **Setup** button within the **File Formats** tab group, select the **Format 1** format method and click on the **<** button to add it to the selected formats.

Configuring An Electronic Payment Method

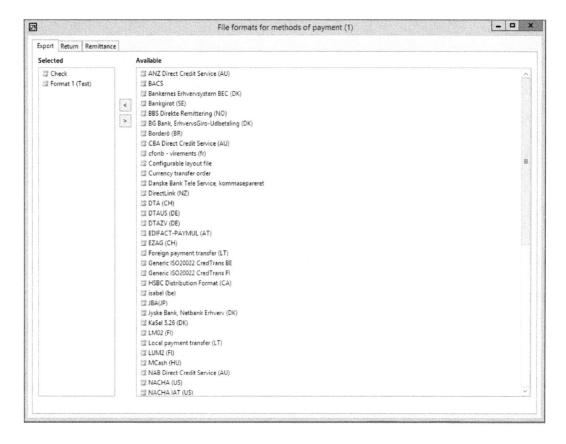

After the **Format 1** format has been added to the **Selected** list you can close out of the form.

Configuring An Electronic Payment Method

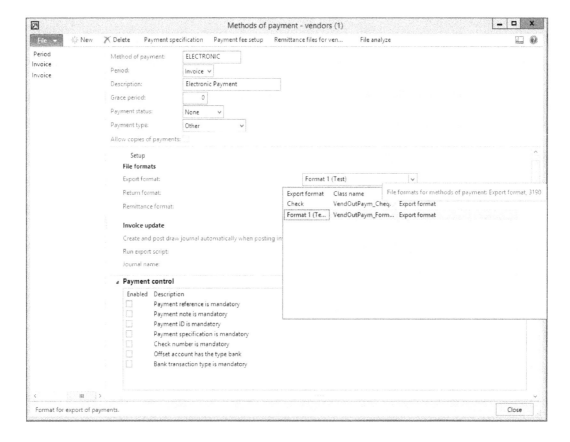

When you return back to the **Methods Of Payments** form you can click on the **Export Format** dropdown list and select the **Format 1** export format.

Configuring An Electronic Payment Method

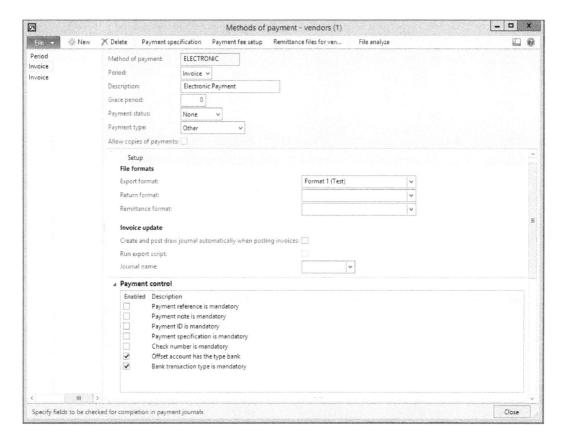

Now expand out the **Payment Control** tab group and check the **Offset Account Has The Type Bank**, and also the **Bank Transaction Type Is Mandatory** flags to add a little control around the check printing.

Configuring An Electronic Payment Method

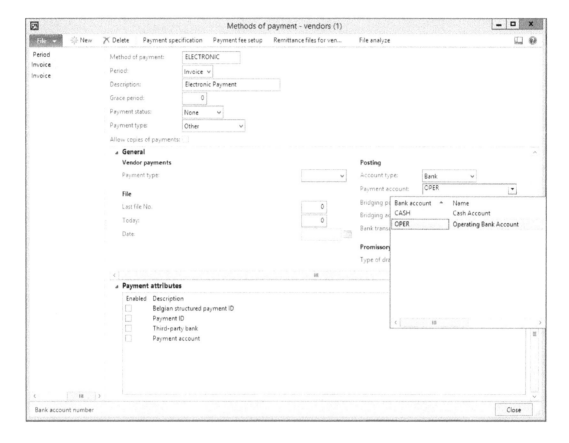

Next open up the **General** tab group, and click on the **Account Type** within the **Posting** field group, select the **Bank** option and then click on the **Payment Account** dropdown list and select the bank account that you want to use by default for the electronic payments.

Configuring An Electronic Payment Method

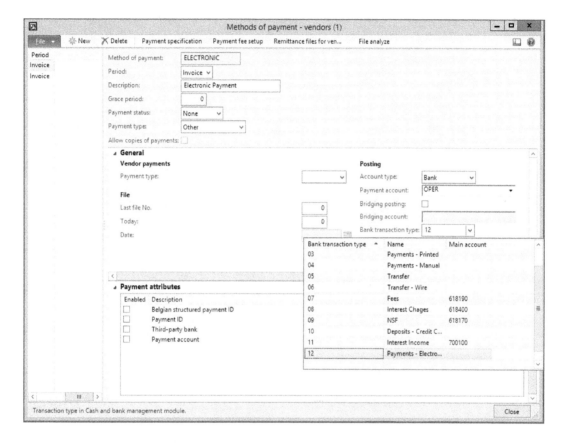

Finally, click on the **Bank Transaction Type** dropdown list and select the default transaction type for the electronic payments – we will use **12**.

Configuring An Electronic Payment Method

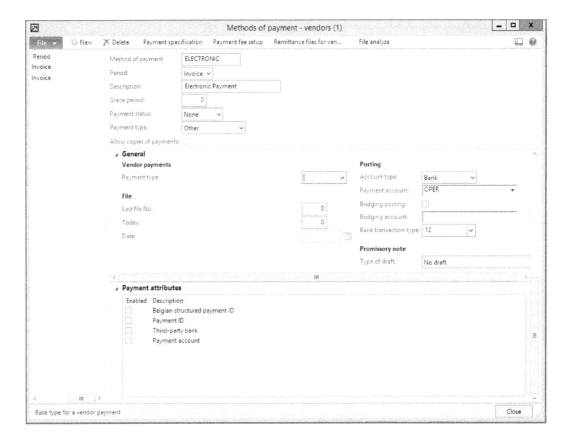

After you have done that you are done with the electronic payment setup.

Configuring A Postdated Check Payment Method

One final type of payment that you may want to configure is for a Postdated Check.

Configuring A Postdated Check Payment Method

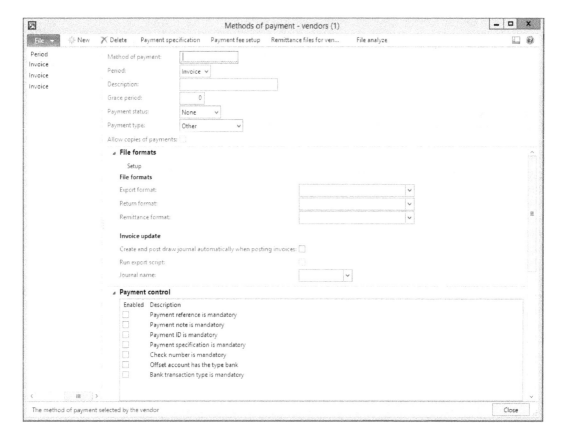

To do this return to the **Methods Of Payments** maintenance form and click on the **New** button within the menu bar to create a new record.

Configuring A Postdated Check Payment Method

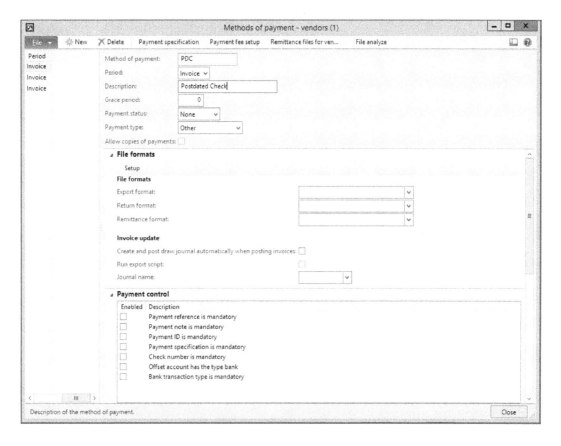

Then set the **Method of Payment** code to **PDC** and the **Description** to **Postdated Check**.

Configuring A Postdated Check Payment Method

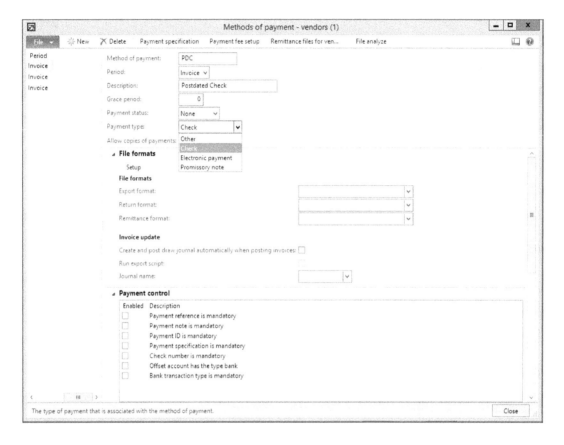

Click on the **Payment Type** dropdown list and select the **Check** option.

Configuring A Postdated Check Payment Method

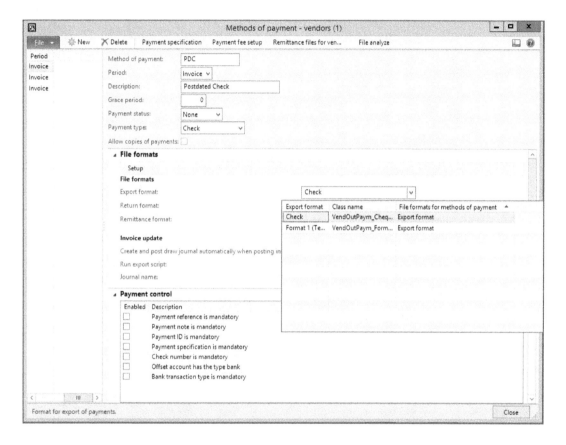

For this payment type we can reuse the export format that we used for the first check payment method by clicking on the dropdown list for the **Export Format** and selecting **Check**.

Configuring A Postdated Check Payment Method

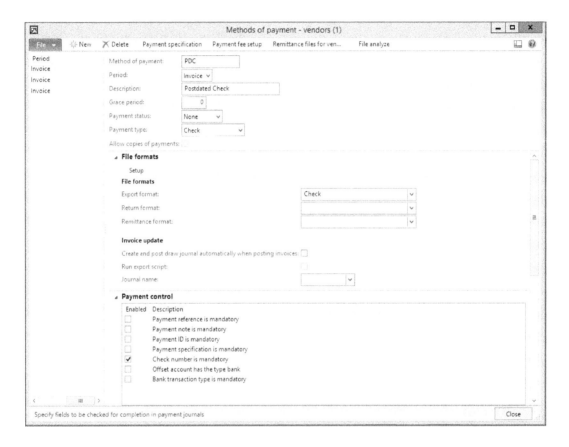

Now expand out the **Payment Control** tab group and check the **Check Number Is Mandatory**, flag.

Configuring A Postdated Check Payment Method

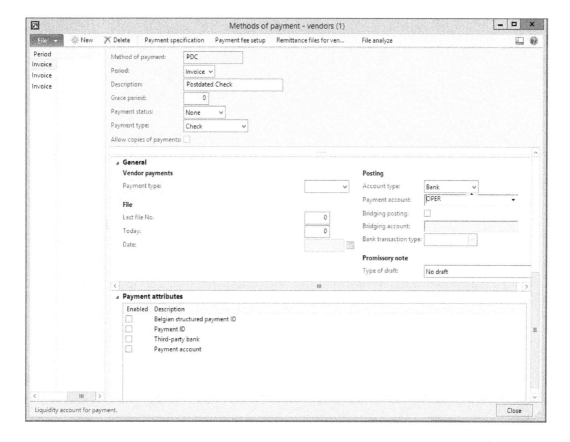

Next open up the **General** tab group, and click on the **Account Type** within the **Posting** field group, select the **Bank** option and then click on the **Payment Account** dropdown list and select the bank account that you want to use by default for the electronic payments.

Configuring A Postdated Check Payment Method

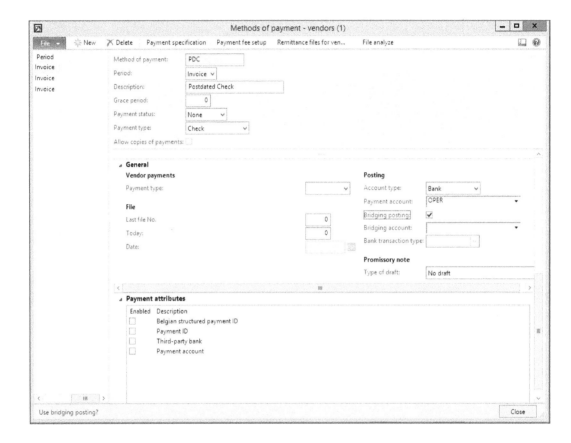

Since this is a postdated check we need a little more information than we had on the original check. We will start off by checking the **Bridging Posting** flag.

Configuring A Postdated Check Payment Method

Then click on the **Bridging Account** dropdown list and select the main account that you want to use for the bridging ledger entries. We will use **211345**.

Finally, click on the **Bank Transaction Type** dropdown list and select the default transaction type for the postdated checks – we will use **04**.

Configuring A Postdated Check Payment Method

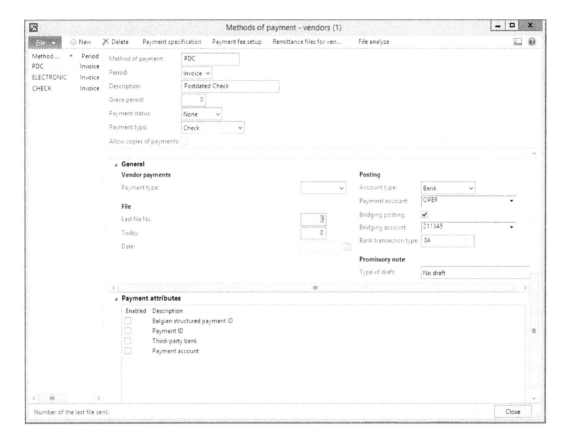

After you have done that you can just click on the **Close** button to exit from the form.

Configuring Accounts Payable Parameters

Now that we have all of the main codes and controls configured we just have a little bit of housekeeping that we need to do and configure a couple of the parameters within the Accounts Payable area.

Configuring Accounts Payable Parameters

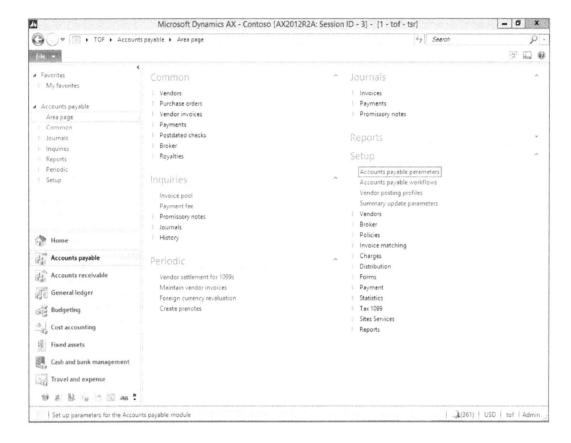

To do this, click on the **Accounts Payable Parameters** menu item within the **Setup** group of the **Accounts Payable** area page.

Configuring Accounts Payable Parameters

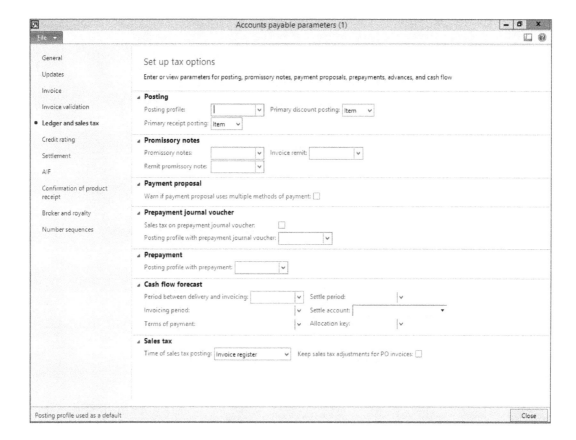

When the **Accounts Payable Parameters** form is displayed, switch to the **Ledger And Sales Tax** page.

Configuring Accounts Payable Parameters

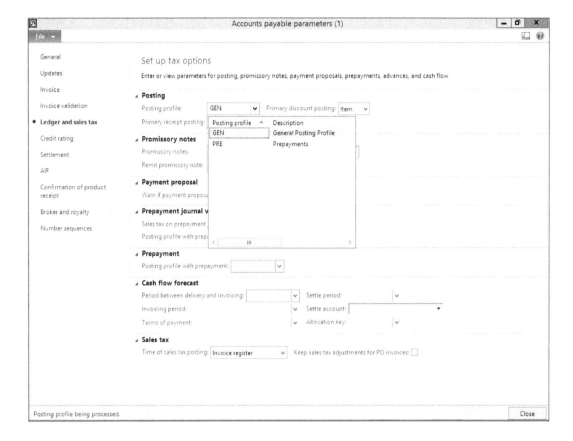

Then click on the **Posting Profile** dropdown list and select your **GEN** posting profile format.

Configuring Accounts Payable Parameters

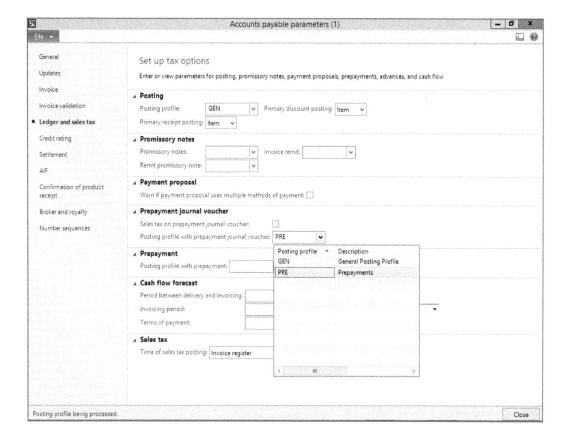

Then click on the dropdown list for the **Posting Profile With Prepayment Journal Voucher** field and select the **PRE** vendor posting profile.

Configuring Accounts Payable Parameters

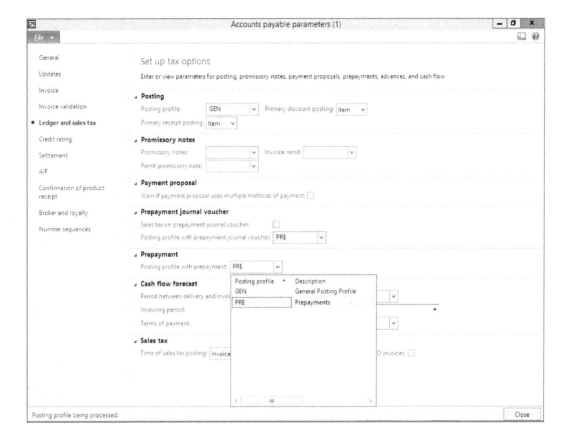

Finally click on the dropdown list for the **Posting Profile With Prepayment** field and select the **PRE** vendor posting profile.

After you have done that, just click on the **Close** button to exit from the form.

CONFIGURING VENDOR ACCOUNTS

Now that you have all of the codes and controls configured you can start adding some real data into the Accounts payable, and the best place to start is by setting up your vendors.

In this chapter we will show you how you can set up individual vendors, and also how you can load in all of your vendors in bulk through the Data Import Export Framework.

Changing the Vendor Numbering Sequence

Before we start though we will make one quick tweak to the system to allow us to use manual numbering for the vendor accounts. You don't have to do this and can have Dynamics AX assign vendor numbers for you automatically, but if you are like most companies you may want to add some of your own intelligence to the numbering format se we need to make the vendor numbering a little more flexible.

Changing the Vendor Numbering Sequence

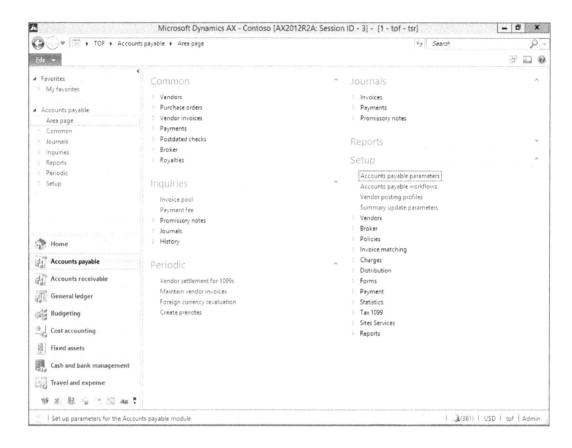

To do this, click on the **Accounts Payable Parameters** menu item within the **Setup** group of the **Accounts Payable** area page.

Changing the Vendor Numbering Sequence

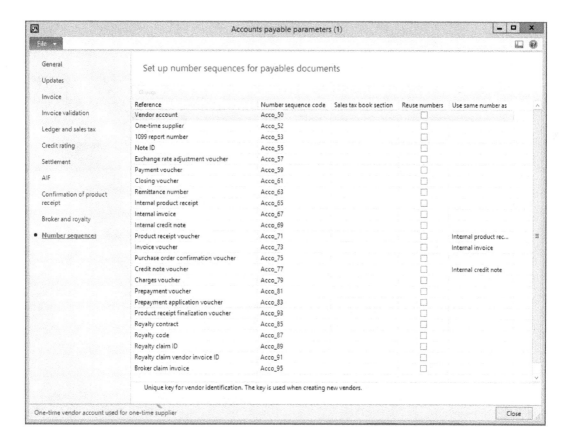

When the **Accounts Payable Parameters** form is displayed, switch to the **Number Sequences** page.

Changing the Vendor Numbering Sequence

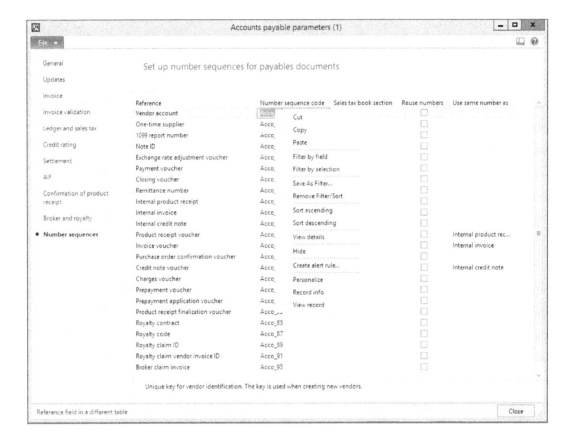

Right-mouse-click on the **Vendor Account** number sequence, and click on the **View Details** menu item.

Changing the Vendor Numbering Sequence

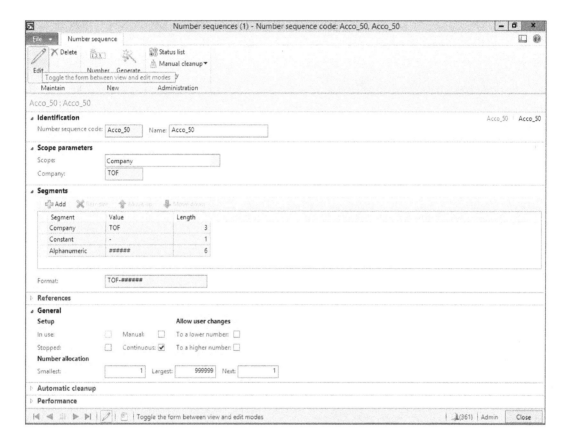

When the **Number Sequence** maintenance form is displayed, click on the **Edit** button within the **Maintain** group of the **Number Sequence** ribbon bar to switch to edit mode.

Changing the Vendor Numbering Sequence

To simplify the vendor number, select the **Company** and **Constant** segments and click the **Remove** button for each of them so that your vendor number format just a numeric value.

Changing the Vendor Numbering Sequence

Then click on the **Manual** flag within the **General** tab group to tell the system that you want to manually assign the vendor numbers.

After you have done that you can just click on the **Close** button to exit from the form.

Configuring Vendor Groups

Before we set up the vendors we need to set up some **Vendor Groups** that you will use to classify your vendors.

Configuring Vendor Groups

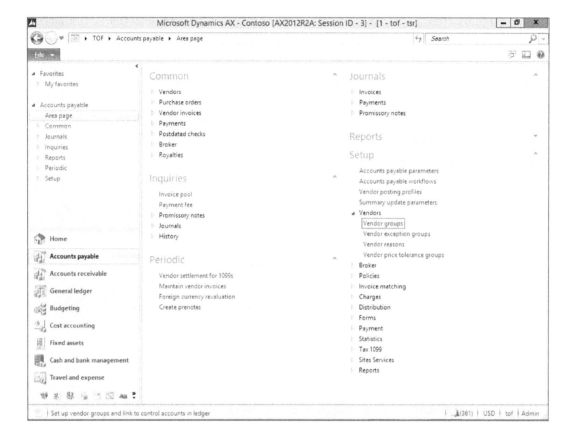

To do this, click on the **Vendor Groups** menu item within the **Vendors** folder of the **Setup** group within the **Accounts Payable** area page.

Configuring Vendor Groups

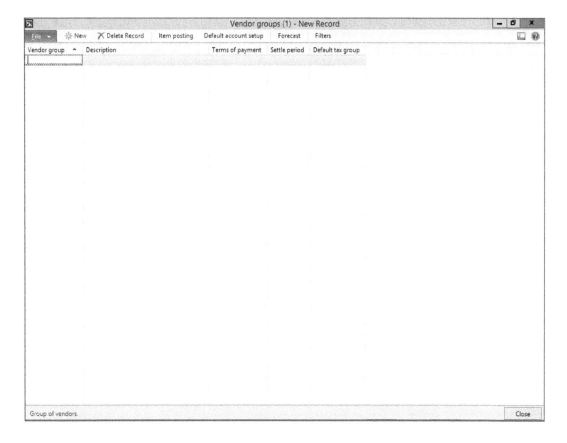

When the **Vendor Groups** maintenance form is displayed, click on the **New** button in the menu bar to create a new record.

Configuring Vendor Groups

Then enter in the **Vendor Group** code and also a **Description.**

Configuring Vendor Groups

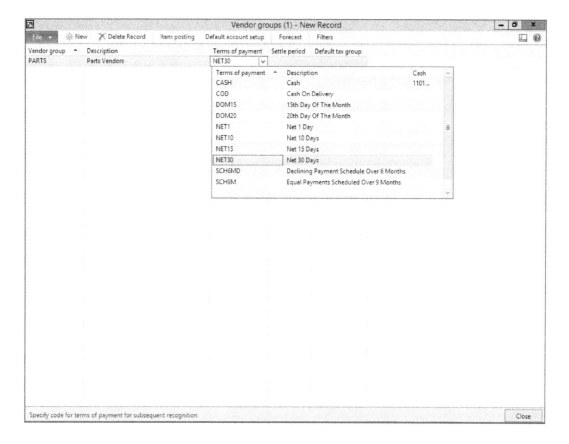

From the **Terms Of Payment** dropdown list, select the default payment terms for the vendor group.

Configuring Vendor Groups

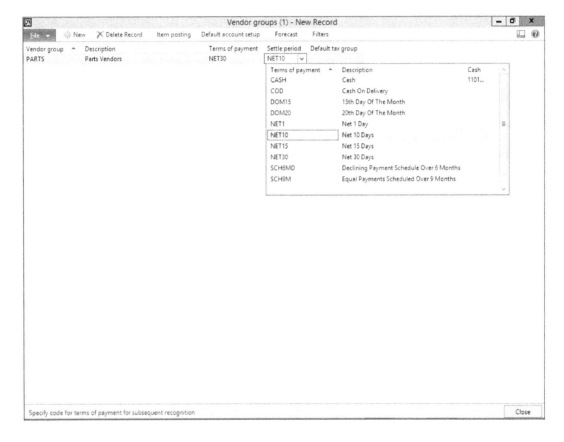

Then click on the **Settle Period** dropdown list and select the default settlement payment terms.

Configuring Vendor Groups

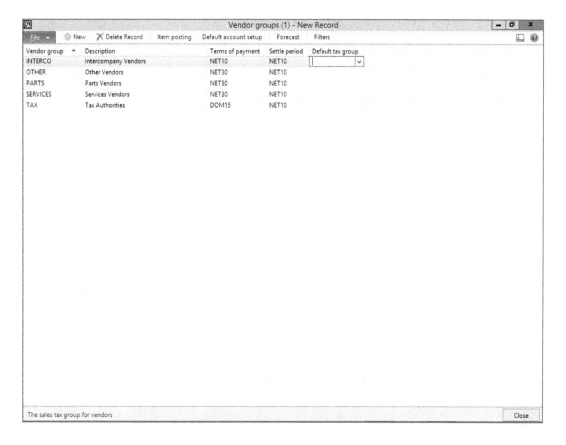

Repeat the process for all of the different groups that you want to use to classify your vendors and then click the **Close** button to exit from the form.

Creating A New Vendor Account

Now we can start adding our vendors.

Creating A New Vendor Account

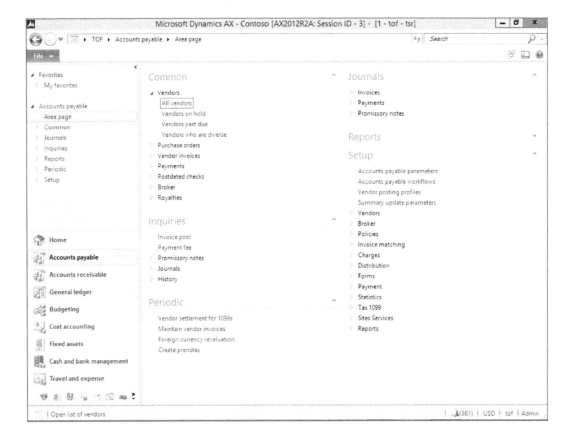

To do this, click on the **All Vendors** menu item within the **Vendors** folder of the **Common** group within the **Accounts Payable** area page.

Creating A New Vendor Account

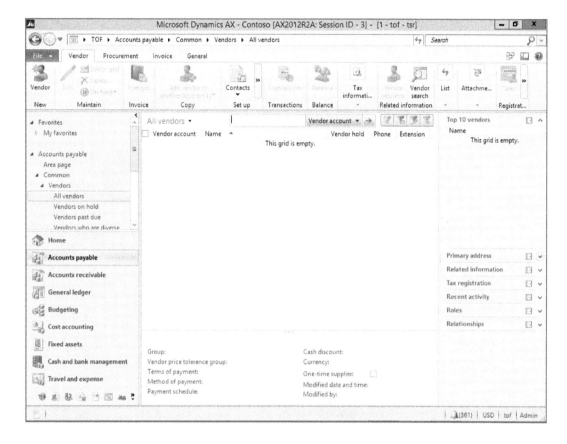

When the **All Vendors** maintenance form is displayed, click on the **Vendor** button within the **New** group of the **Vendor** ribbon bar.

Creating A New Vendor Account

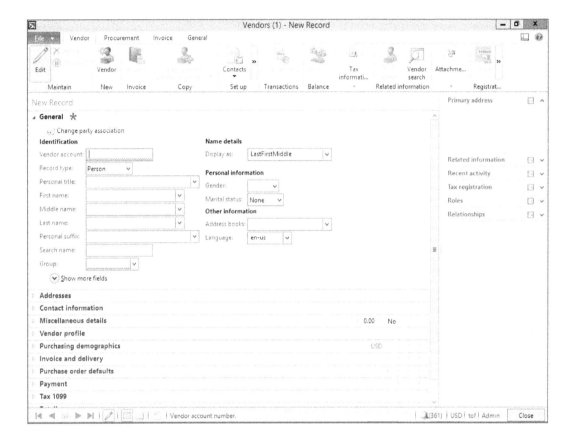

This will open up a new **Vendors** maintenance form.

Creating A New Vendor Account

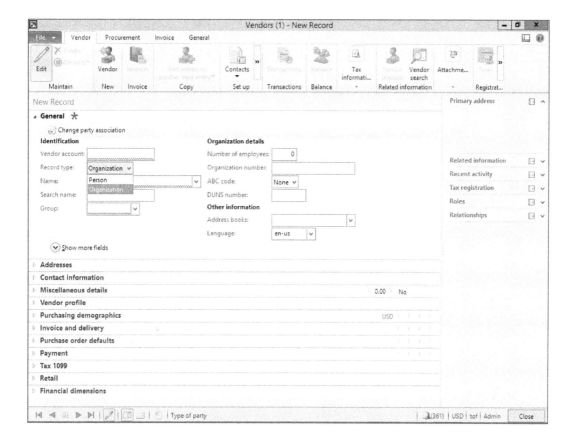

Vendors can either be an individual or an organizations within Dynamics AX. By default the record type is **Organization** but if you want to set up a person, then click on the **Record Type** dropdown list and you will be able to select the type of party that you will create for the vendor.

Creating A New Vendor Account

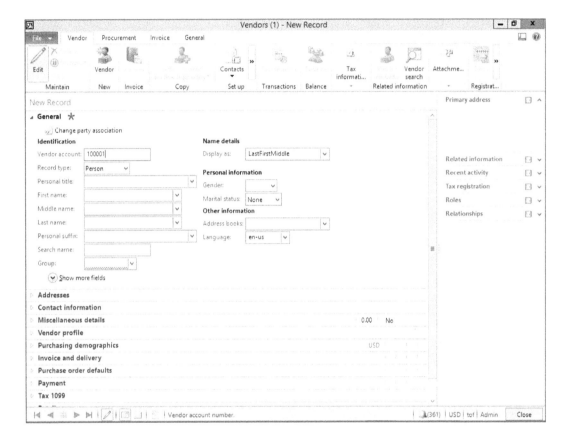

If you select the **Person** option then you will notice that the naming conventions change to be more person related.

Creating A New Vendor Account

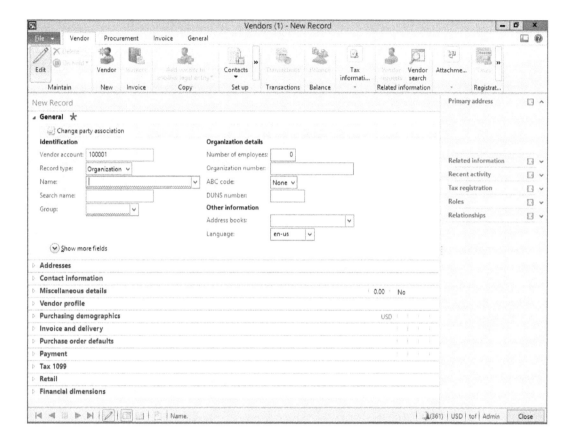

If you change it to an Organization then you have a little less information.

Set the **Record Type** to **Organization** and then set the **Vendor Account** number that you want to use.

Creating A New Vendor Account

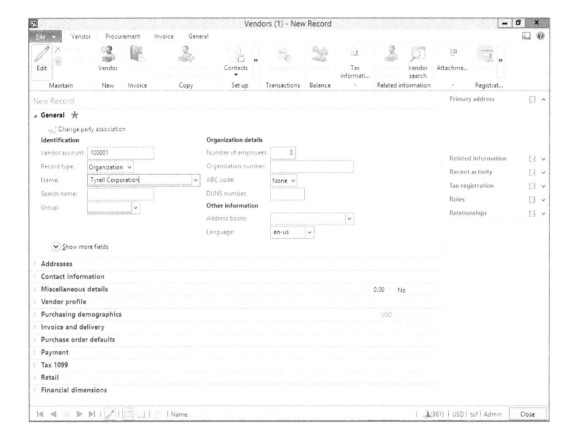

Then type in the **Name** of the organization.

Creating A New Vendor Account

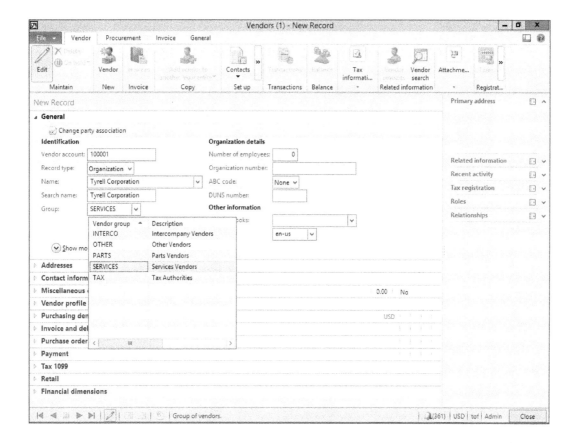

Next, click on the dropdown list for the **Group** field and select the **Vendor Group** that you want to assign to this vendor.

Creating A New Vendor Account

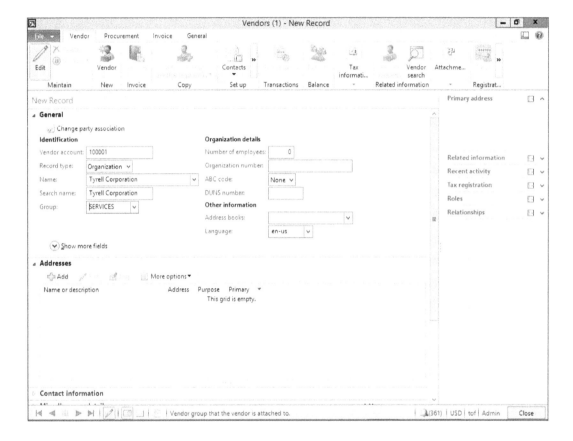

Now expand out the **Addresses** tab group and you will notice that there are no default address details for the vendor. To fix this click on the **Add** button within the grids menu bar.

Creating A New Vendor Account

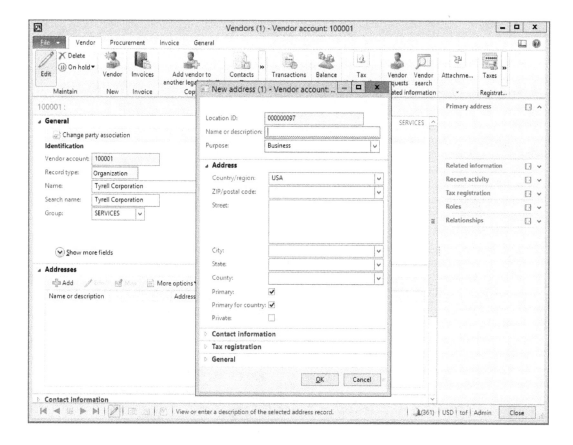

This will open up a **New Address** dialog box.

Creating A New Vendor Account

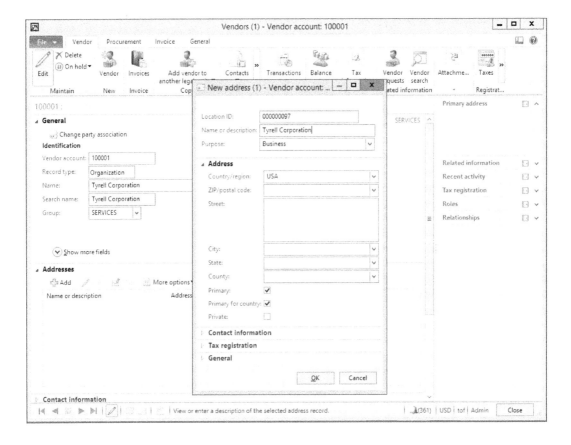

Type in a **Name or Description** for the address.

Creating A New Vendor Account

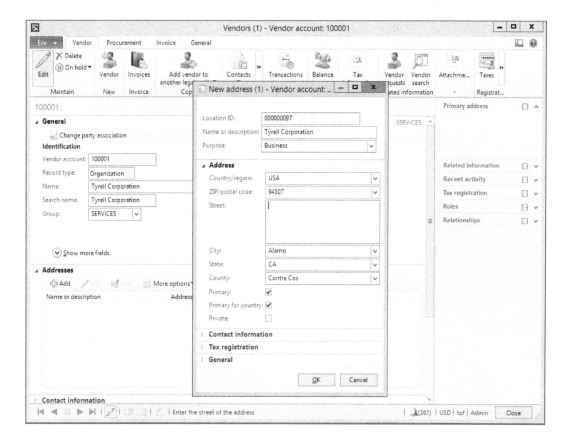

Then type in the **Zip/Postal Code** for the address. Notice that it also fills in all of the **City**, **State** and **County** information for you.

Creating A New Vendor Account

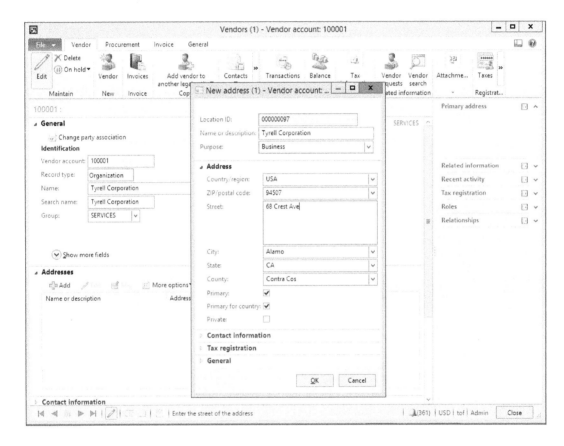

Then type in the **Street** address and when you are done, click on the **OK** button to save the address.

Creating A New Vendor Account

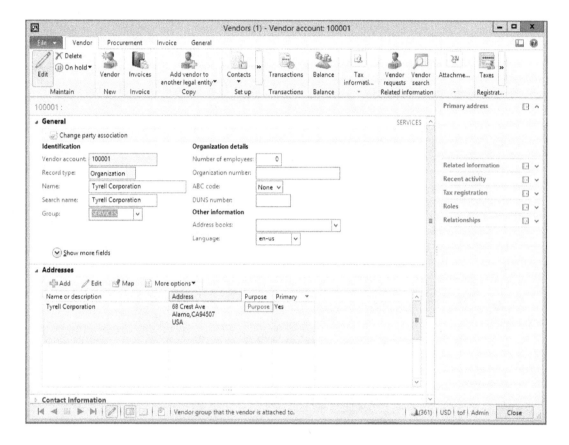

Now you will see that the address has been added to your vendor account.

Creating A New Vendor Account

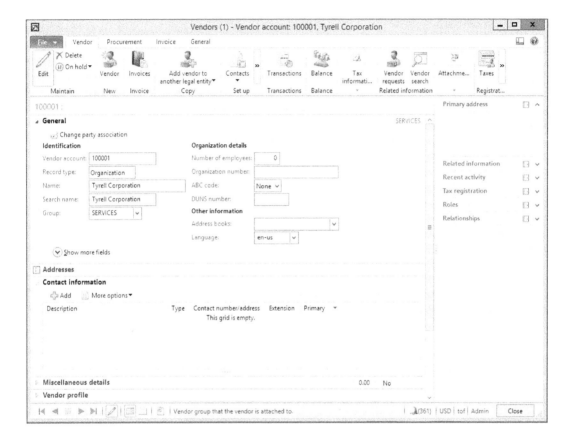

Now expand out the **Contact Information** tab group.

Creating A New Vendor Account

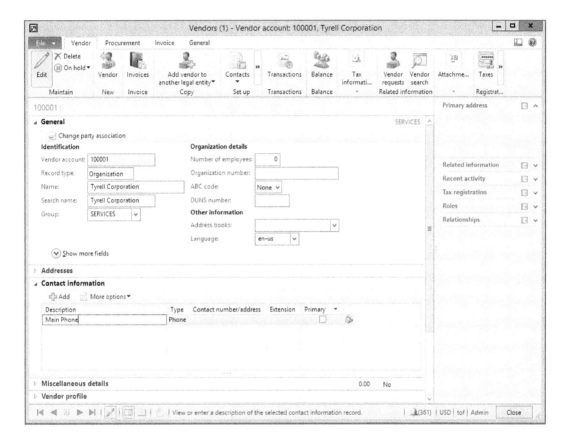

Click on the **Add** button in the grids menu bar to create a new record, and enter in a **Description**.

Creating A New Vendor Account

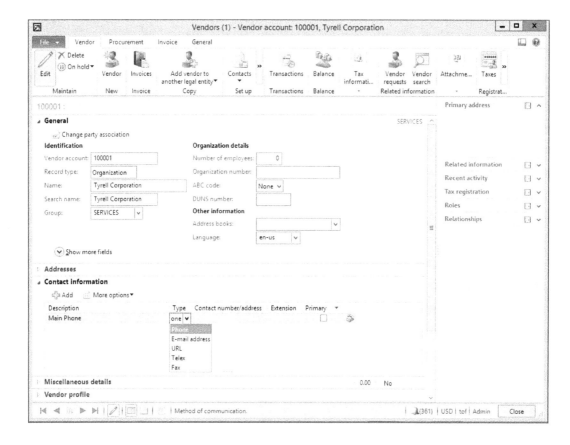

Click on the **Type** dropdown list and select the type of contact information you are adding – i.e. **Phone**, **e-Mail**, **URL** etc.

Creating A New Vendor Account

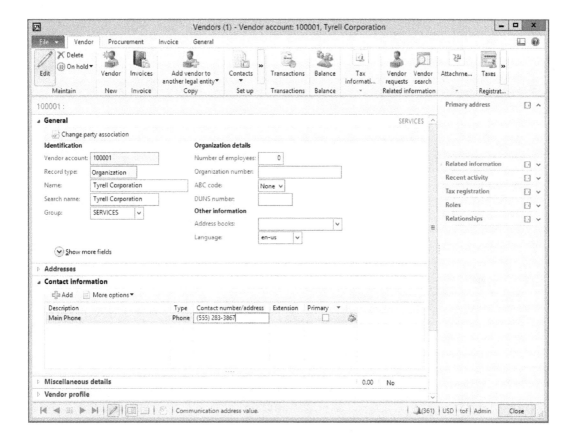

And then type in the **Contact Number/Address**.

Creating A New Vendor Account

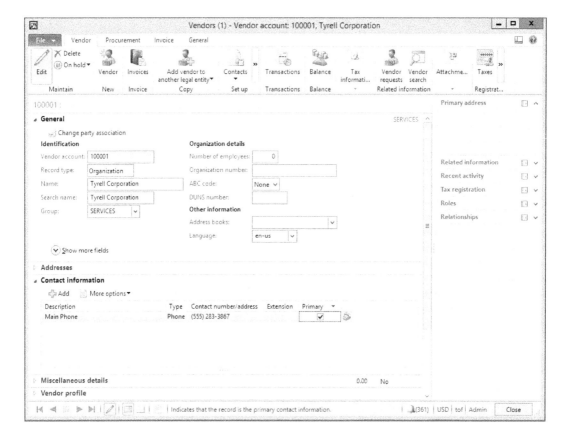

If you want this to be the default for this type of contact then you can check the **Primary** flag for the record.

Creating A New Vendor Account

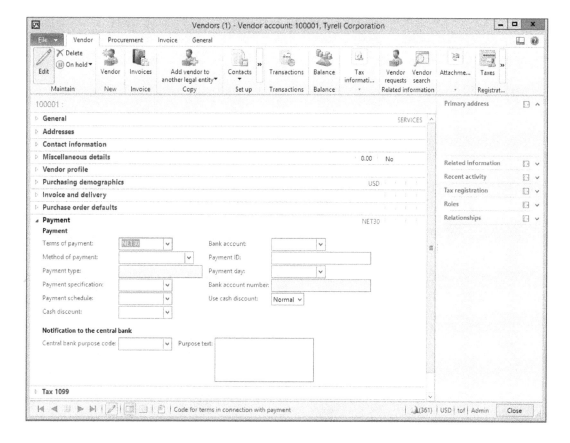

Now expand the **Payment** tab group and you will see that there is a lot more information here that you can configure for the vendor, and that some of the information has already been defaulted in off the vendor group.

Creating A New Vendor Account

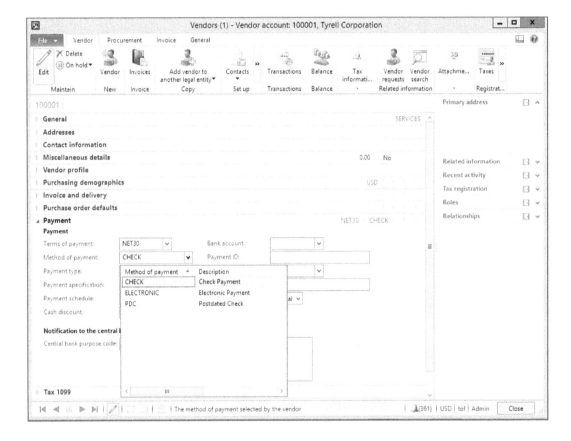

Click on the dropdown list for the **Method of Payment** and select the default way that you will pay the vendor – we will select **CHECK**.

After you have done that then you can just click the **Close** button and exit from the form.

Creating A New Vendor Account

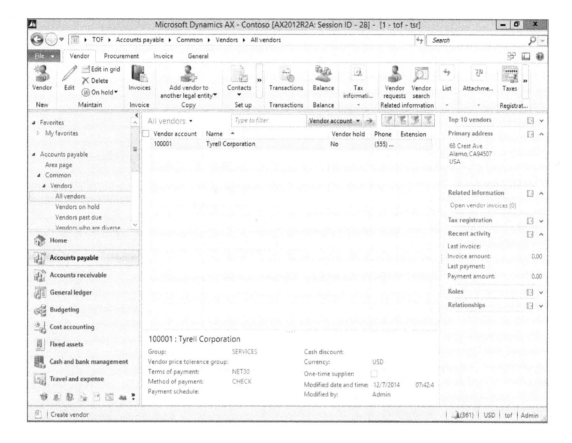

Now when you return back to the **All Vendors** list page you will see that you have a vendor record that you can start using.

Importing Vendors Using The Data Import Export Framework

Adding vendors one at a time is good, but if you have a lot of vendors that you want to load into Dynamics AX then you may want to use the **Data Import Export Framework** to load them all in from a CSV file.

Importing Vendors Using The Data Import Export Framework

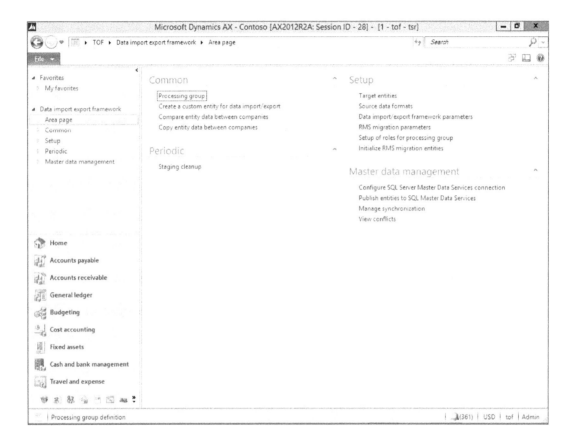

To do this click on the **Processing Group** menu item within the **Common** group of the **Data Import Export Framework** area page.

Importing Vendors Using The Data Import Export Framework

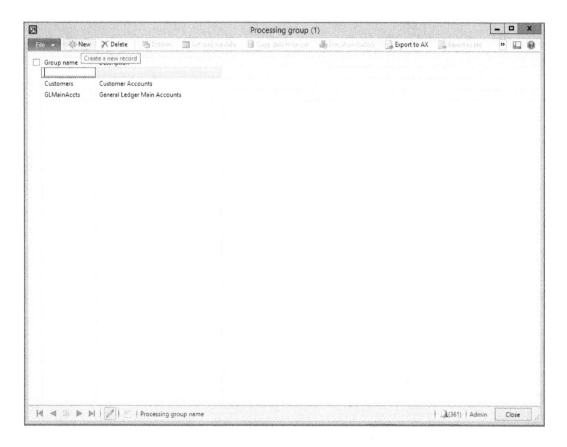

When the **Processing Group** maintenance form is displayed, click on the **New** button within the menu bar to create a new record.

Importing Vendors Using The Data Import Export Framework

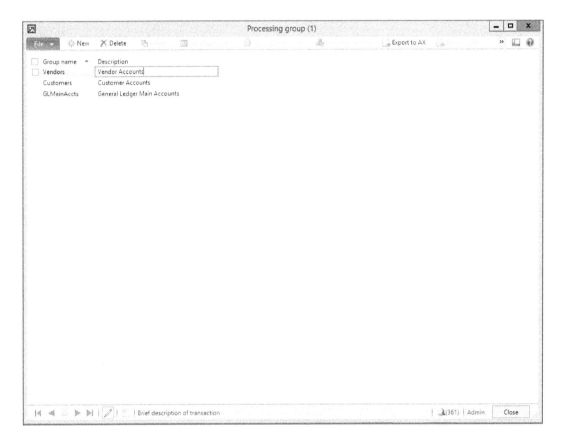

Set the **Group Name** to **Vendors** and the **Description** to **Vendor Accounts.**

Importing Vendors Using The Data Import Export Framework

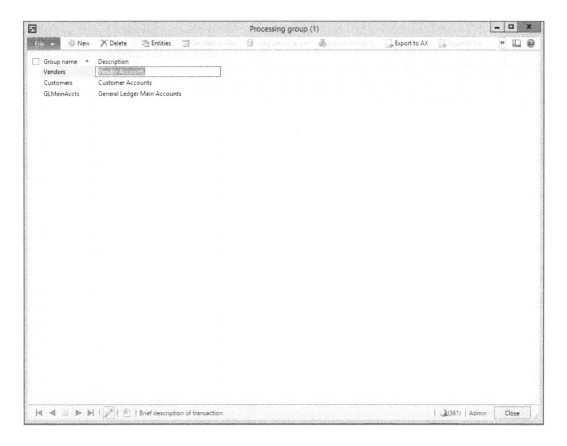

Press **CTRL+S** to save the record and you will notice that the **Entities** button in the menu bar becomes enabled and you can then click on it.

Importing Vendors Using The Data Import Export Framework

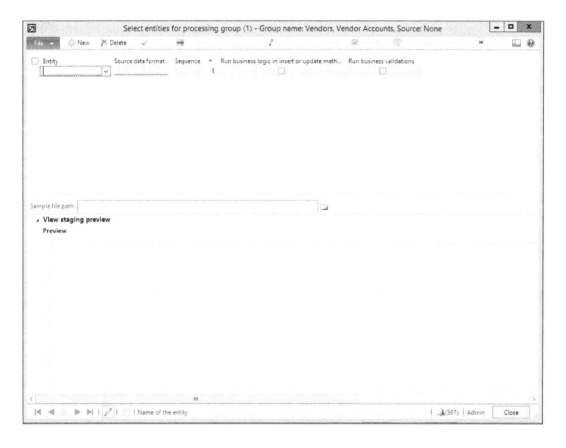

When the **Select Entities For Processing Group** form is displayed, click on the **New** button in the menu bar to create a new record.

Importing Vendors Using The Data Import Export Framework

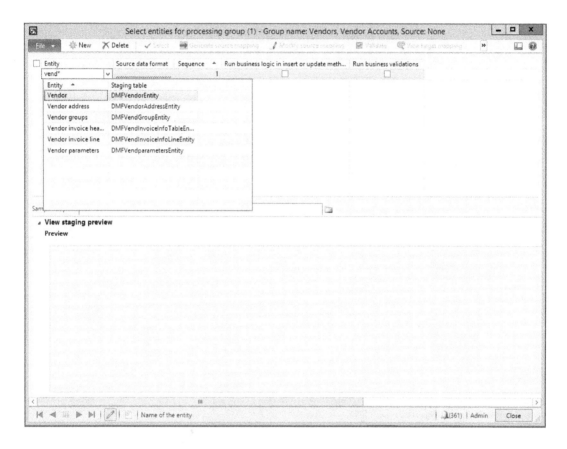

Then click on the **Entity** dropdown list and select the **Vendor** entity.

Importing Vendors Using The Data Import Export Framework

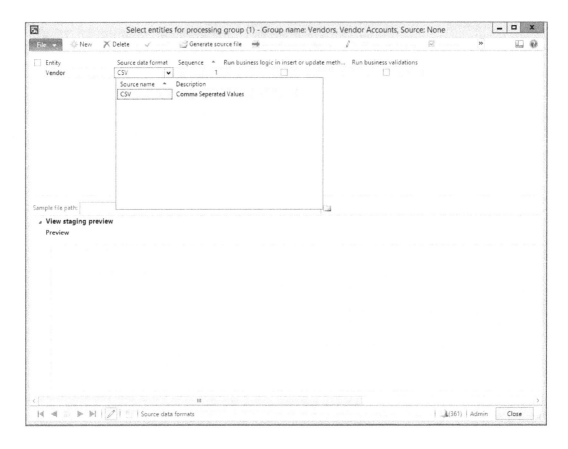

Click on the **Source File** dropdown list and select the **CSV** record.

Importing Vendors Using The Data Import Export Framework

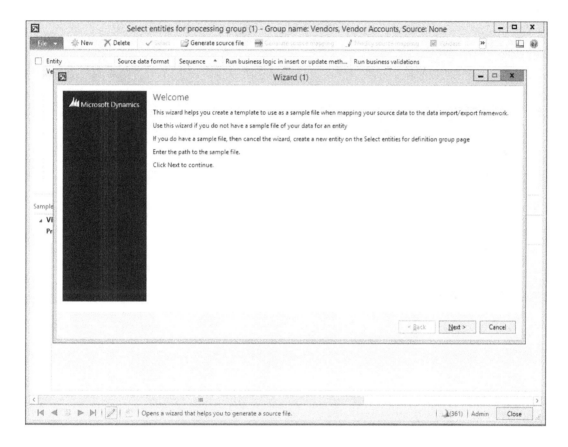

Then click on the **Generate Source File** button in the menu bar.

When the wizard is displayed, click on the **Next** button.

Importing Vendors Using The Data Import Export Framework

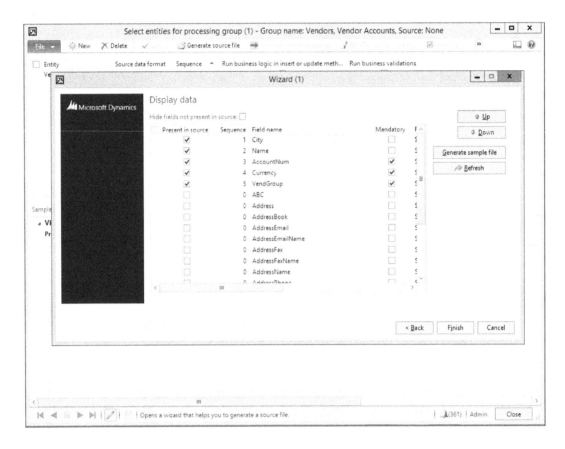

This will take you to the **Display Data** page where you will see all f the fields that are available for import, and also the ones that have been selected by default.

Importing Vendors Using The Data Import Export Framework

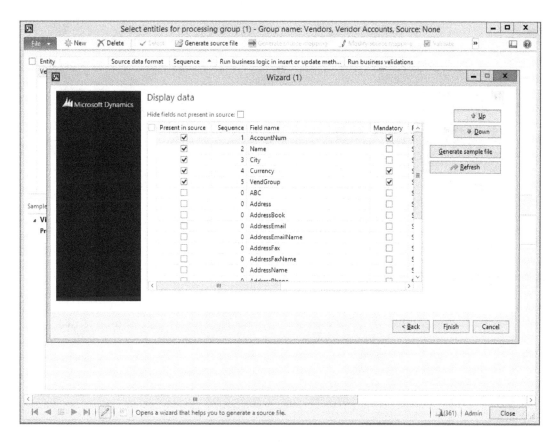

If you select the **AccountNum** field then you can use the **Up** button to move it to the top of the form.

Importing Vendors Using The Data Import Export Framework

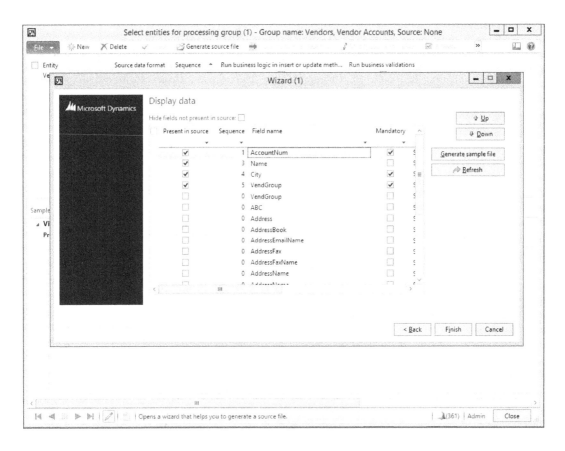

Now we will add a couple more fields to the import. Rather than scrolling down though to find the fields, press **CTRL+G** to turn on the grid search bar.

Importing Vendors Using The Data Import Export Framework

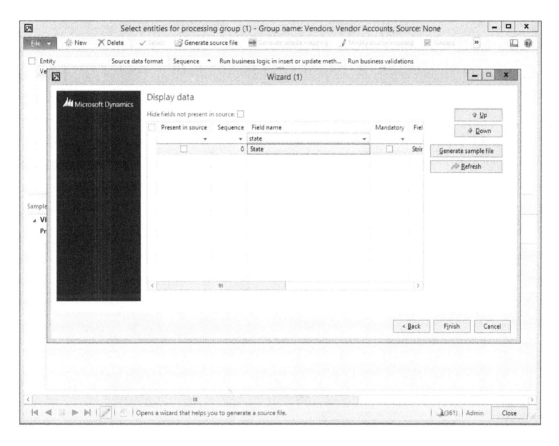

Type in **State** into the **Field Name** search field to find the state.

Importing Vendors Using The Data Import Export Framework

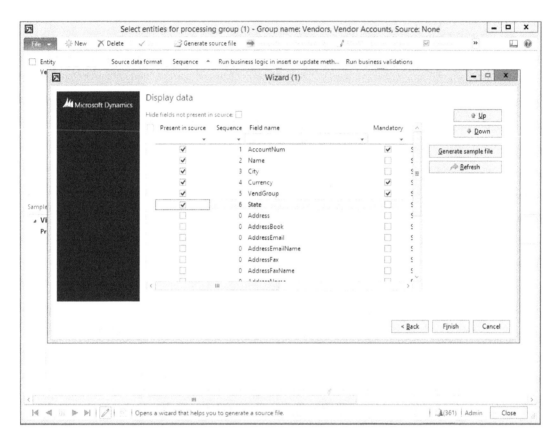

Then click on the **Present In Source** checkbox and the state will be added to the list of default fields.

Importing Vendors Using The Data Import Export Framework

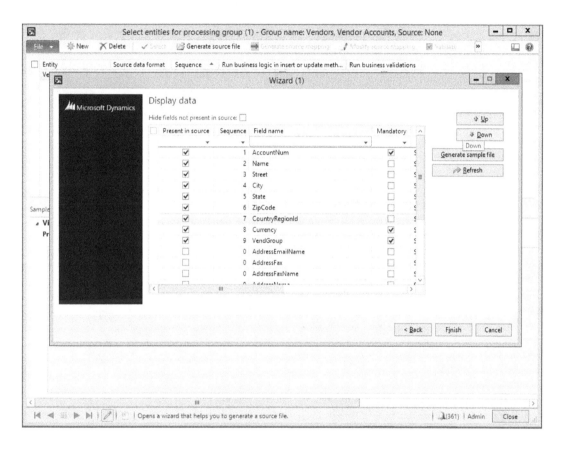

Repeat this process to add in the **Street**, **City**, **Zip Code**, and also **CountryRegionID**.

Then you may also want to rearrange the fields a little so that they are in a better order.

When you are done, click on the **Generate Sample File** button.

Importing Vendors Using The Data Import Export Framework

This will create a text file for you with all of the field headings.

Importing Vendors Using The Data Import Export Framework

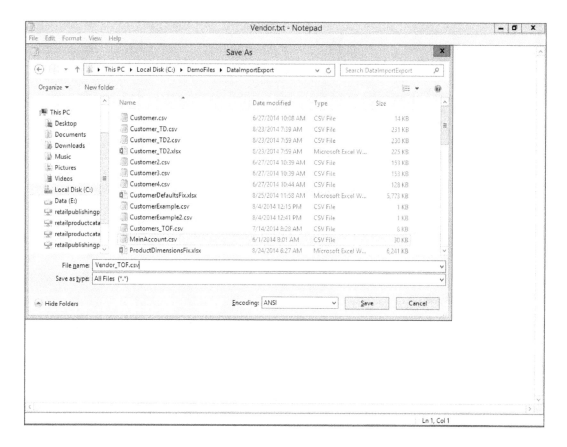

Save the file away as a **.csv** file.

Importing Vendors Using The Data Import Export Framework

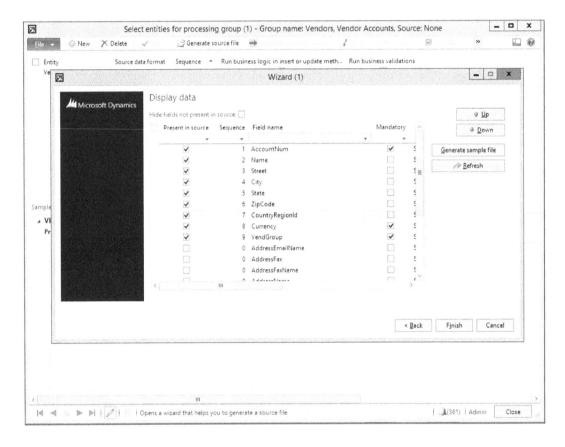

After you have done that, click on the **Finish** button to exit from the wizard.

Importing Vendors Using The Data Import Export Framework

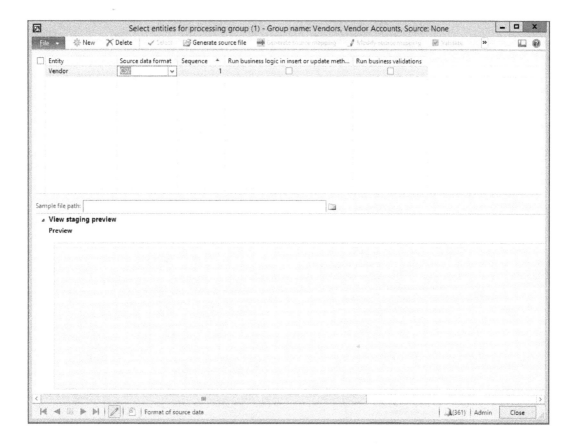

When you return back to the entities form, click on the folder icon to the right of the **Sample File Path** field.

Importing Vendors Using The Data Import Export Framework

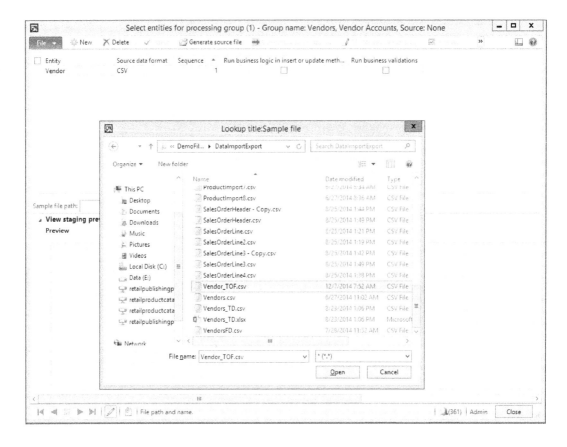

This will allow you to navigate to the csv template that you just created through the wizard, and click the **Open** button to select it.

Importing Vendors Using The Data Import Export Framework

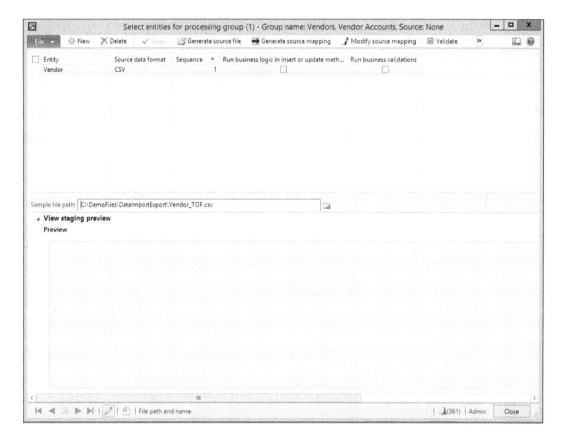

This will add the file path into the **Sample File Path** field.

Importing Vendors Using The Data Import Export Framework

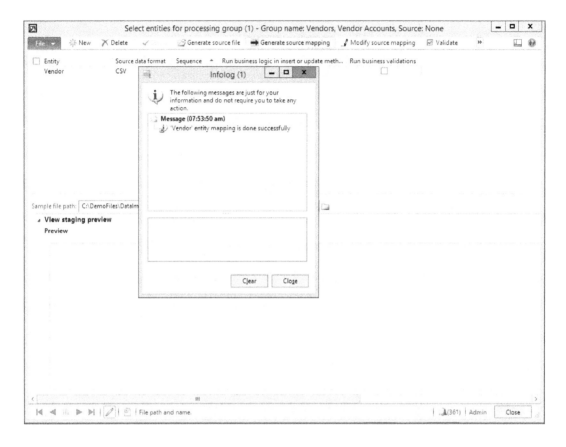

Now click on the **Generate Source Mapping** button in the menu bar to create the default mapping between the data in the CSV file and Dynamics AX.

Importing Vendors Using The Data Import Export Framework

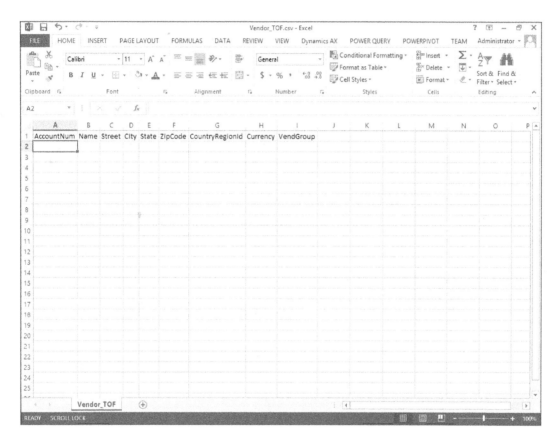

Now find the CSV file and open it up in Excel.

Importing Vendors Using The Data Import Export Framework

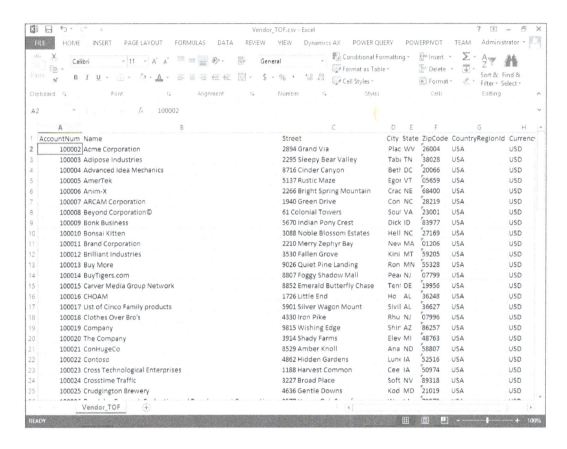

This will allow you to paste all of your vendor details into the spreadsheet and save it back as a CSV file.

Importing Vendors Using The Data Import Export Framework

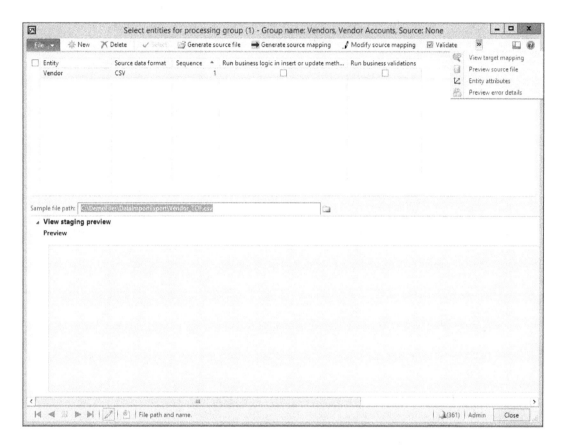

To test the data that you have loaded in the file, click on the **Preview Source File** button within the menu bar.

Importing Vendors Using The Data Import Export Framework

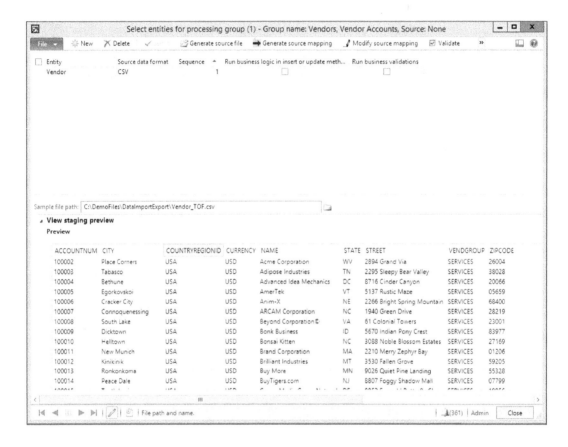

Within the **View Staging Preview** tab group you should see all of the vendor records that you copied over into the CSV file.

If everything looks good then click on the **Close** button to exit from the form.

Importing Vendors Using The Data Import Export Framework

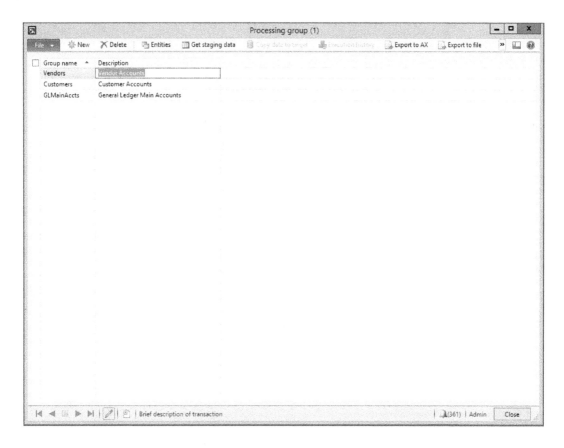

When you return to the **Processing Group** form, click on the **Get Staging Data** button within then menu bar to start the data import.

Importing Vendors Using The Data Import Export Framework

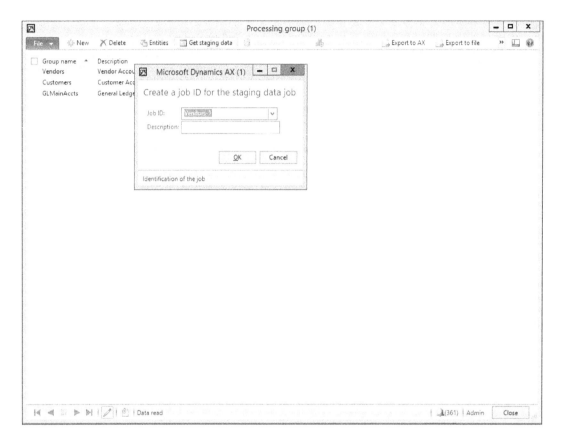

This will open up a dialog box for the job, and all you need to do is click on the **OK** button.

Importing Vendors Using The Data Import Export Framework

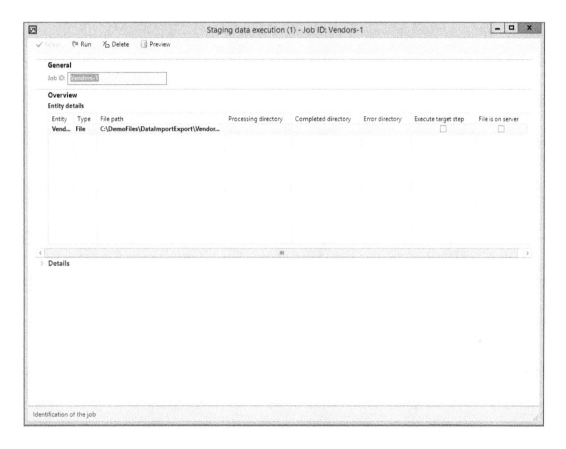

When the **Staging Data Execution** form is displayed, you can double check the data by clicking on the **Preview** button in the menu bar.

Importing Vendors Using The Data Import Export Framework

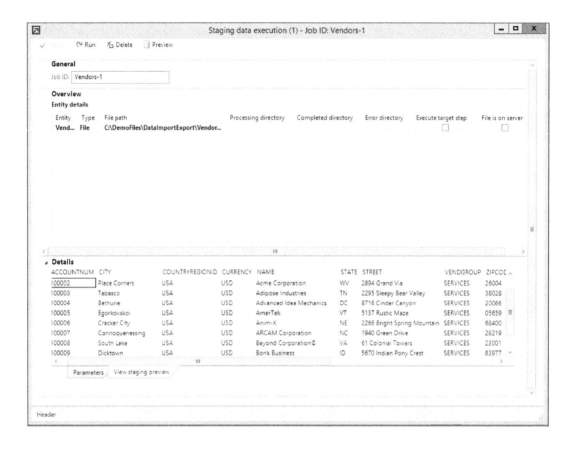

If you expand out the **Details** tab group then you should see all of your vendors are loaded into the data preview section.

Importing Vendors Using The Data Import Export Framework

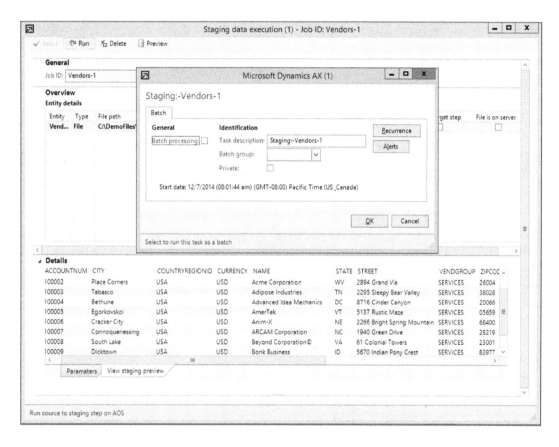

Now click on the **Run** button within the menu bar.

This will open up a staging dialog box – all you need to do is click on the **OK** button.

Importing Vendors Using The Data Import Export Framework

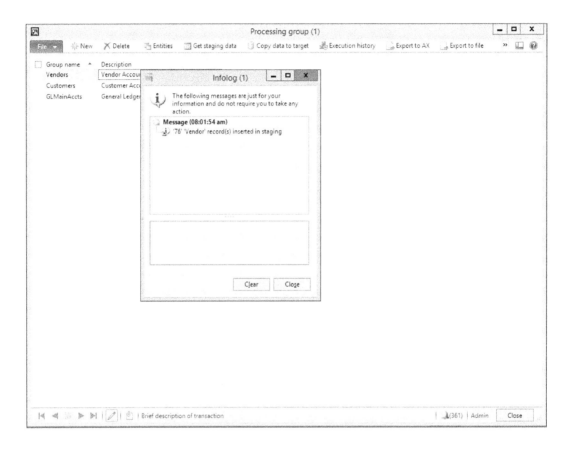

If everything works and there are no errors in the data then you will see an InfoLog message saying that the records were loaded.

Importing Vendors Using The Data Import Export Framework

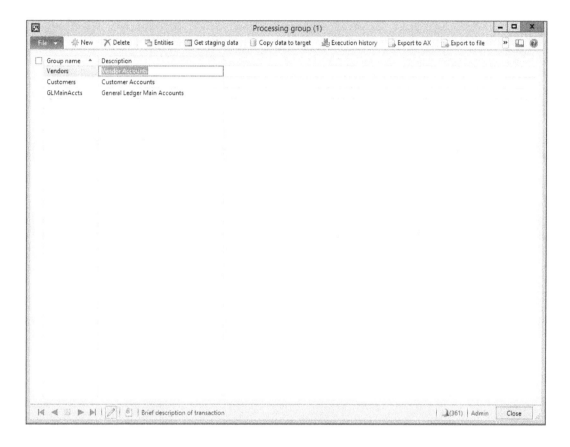

Now you will be able to click on the **Copy Data To Target** button in the menu bar.

Importing Vendors Using The Data Import Export Framework

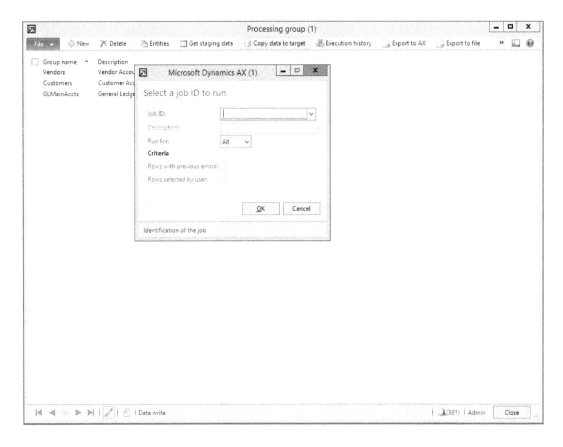

This will open up a job selection dialog box.

Importing Vendors Using The Data Import Export Framework

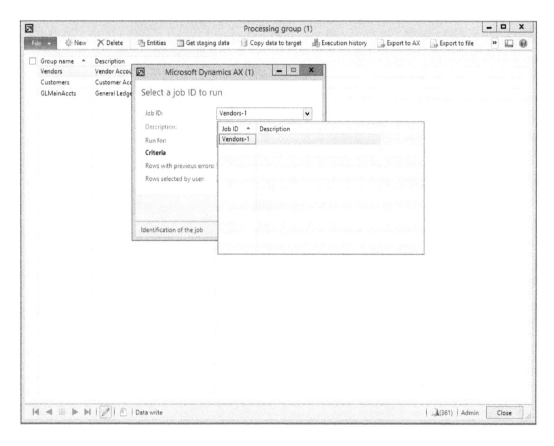

Click on the **Job ID** dropdown list and select the job that you just created in the previous step.

Importing Vendors Using The Data Import Export Framework

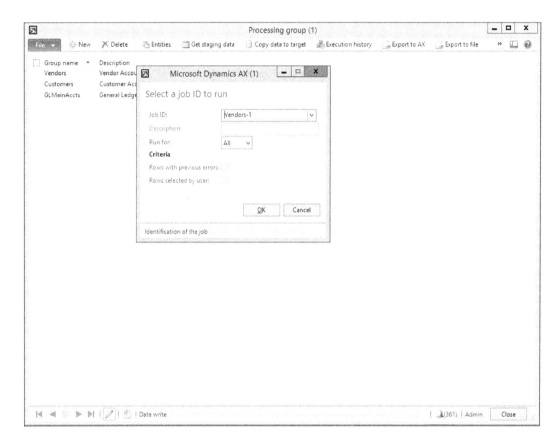

Then click the **OK** button.

Importing Vendors Using The Data Import Export Framework

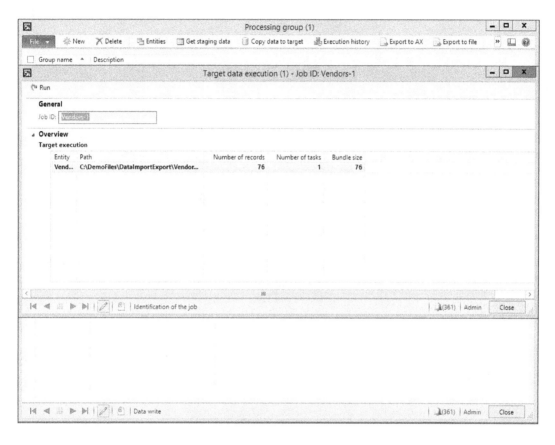

This will open up a **Target Data Execution** dialog box. To start the data load process just click on the **Run** button.

Importing Vendors Using The Data Import Export Framework

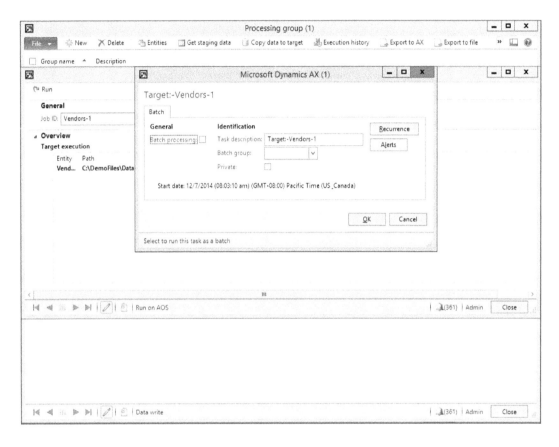

When the execution dialog box is displayed, click on the **OK** button.

Importing Vendors Using The Data Import Export Framework

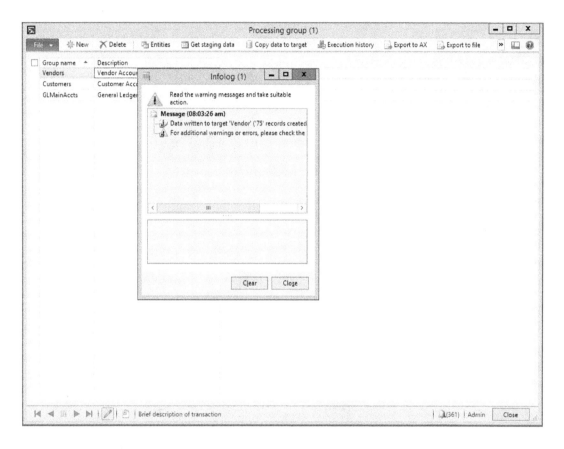

You will then get a message telling you how many of the records were imported and you can click on the **Close** button to exit from the form.

Importing Vendors Using The Data Import Export Framework

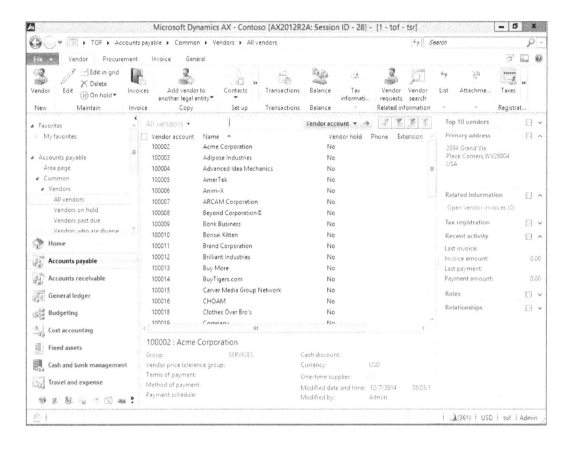

When you return back to your **All Vendors** list page you will see that all of your vendors have now been loaded in.

Importing Vendors Using The Data Import Export Framework

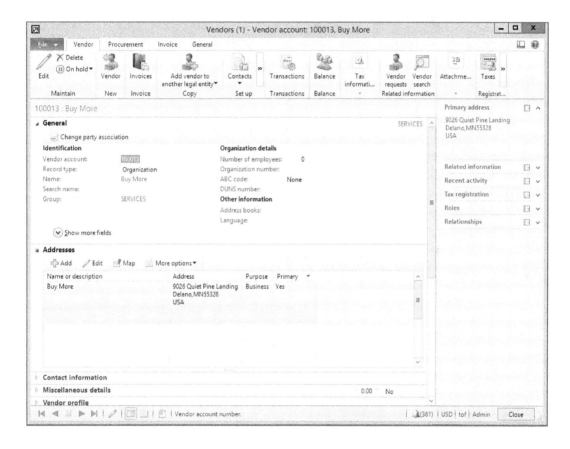

If you open any of them up then you will see that all of the address data has been loaded in as well.

How easy is that!

Updating Vendor Information Manually

Once you have the vendors loaded in, you may want to make a couple of tweaks to them just to polish up the data. One of the ways you can do this is through the vendor card itself.

Updating Vendor Information Manually

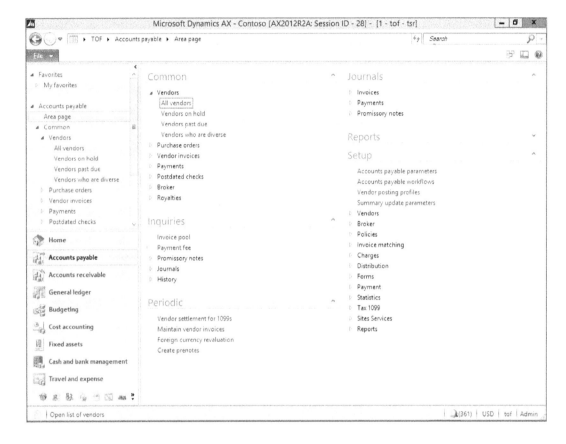

To do this, click on the **All Vendors** within the **Vendors** folder of the **Common** group within the **Accounts Payable** area page.

Updating Vendor Information Manually

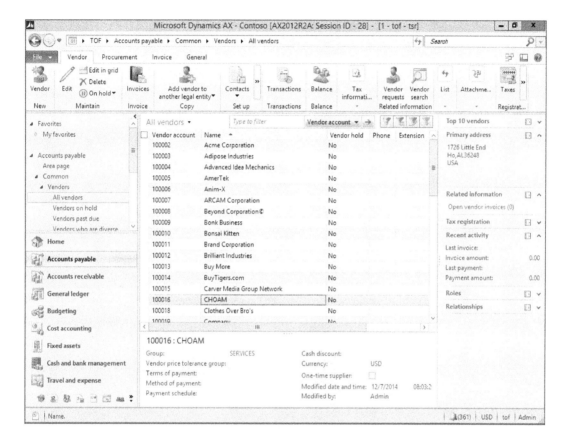

When the **All Vendors** list page is displayed, just double click on the record that you want to modify.

Updating Vendor Information Manually

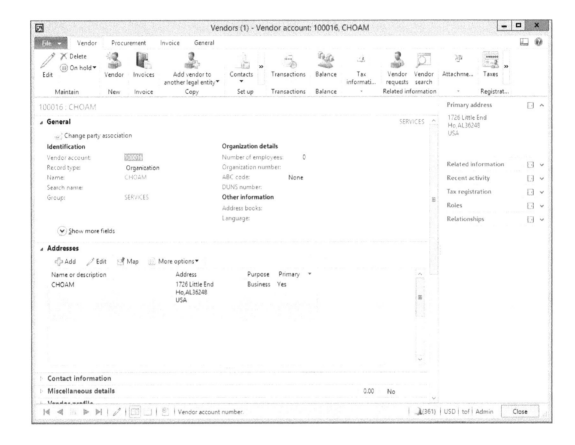

This will open up the vendor details for you.

Updating Vendor Information Manually

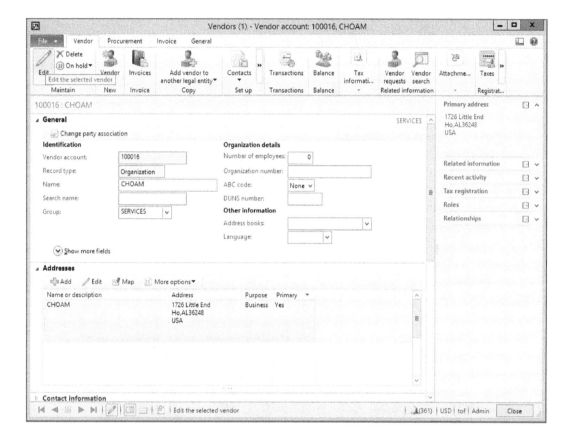

If you click on the **Edit** button within the **Maintain** group of the **Vendors** ribbon bar then you will notice that you can toggle from display to edit mode.

Updating Vendor Information Manually

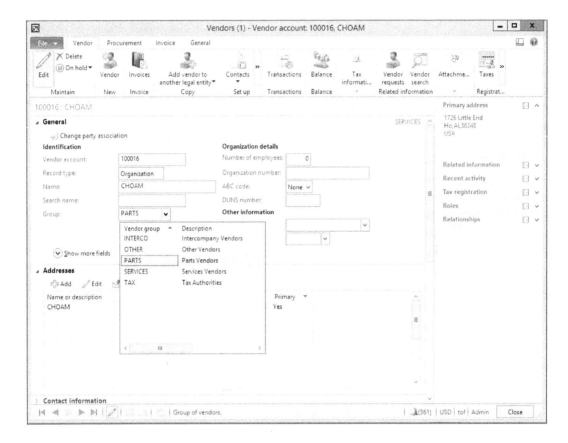

You van then update any of the fields you like.

Updating Vendor Information Manually

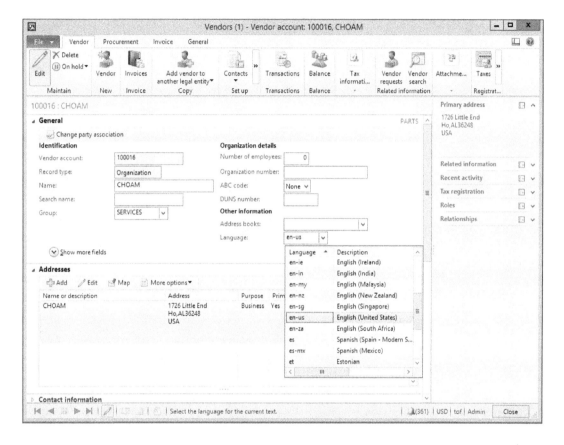

One that you may want to change is the **Language** code.

Updating Vendor Information Manually

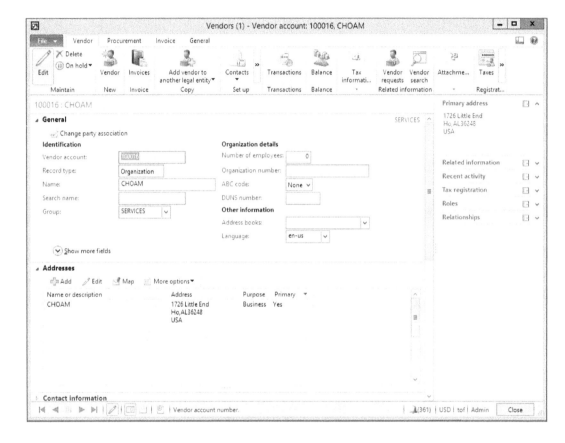

After you have made the changes that you want you can just click on the **Close** button to exit from the form.

Performing Bulk Updates Using The Edit In Grid Function

Another way that you can make updates to the data is through the **Edit In Grid** feature that is built into the vendor maintenance form.

Performing Bulk Updates Using The Edit In Grid Function

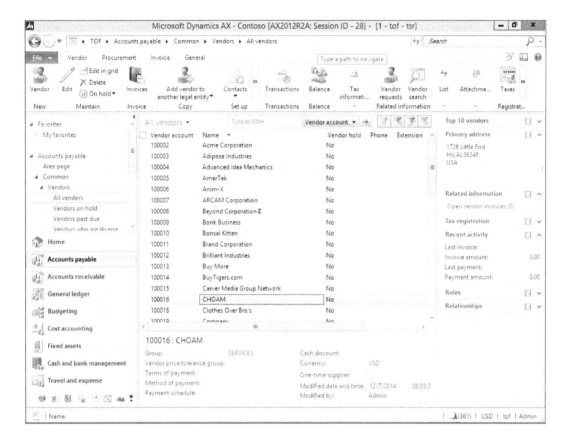

To do this, open up the **All Vendors** list page and then click on the **Edit In Grid** button within the **Maintain** group of the **Vendors** ribbon bar.

Performing Bulk Updates Using The Edit In Grid Function

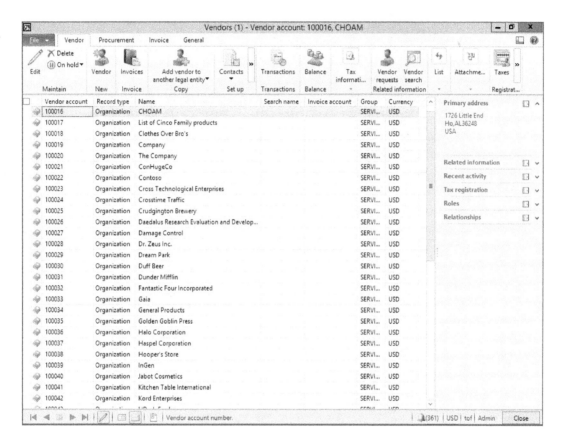

This will open up the vendors in a new view that acts more like a spreadsheet.

Performing Bulk Updates Using The Edit In Grid Function

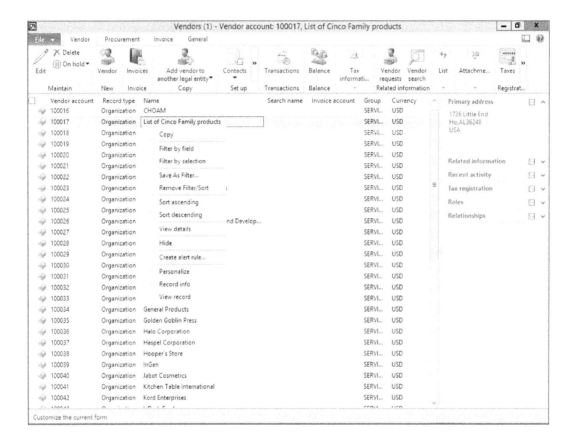

If you want to update fields that are not already on the grid, then right-mouse-click on any of the fields and select the **Personalize** menu item.

Performing Bulk Updates Using The Edit In Grid Function

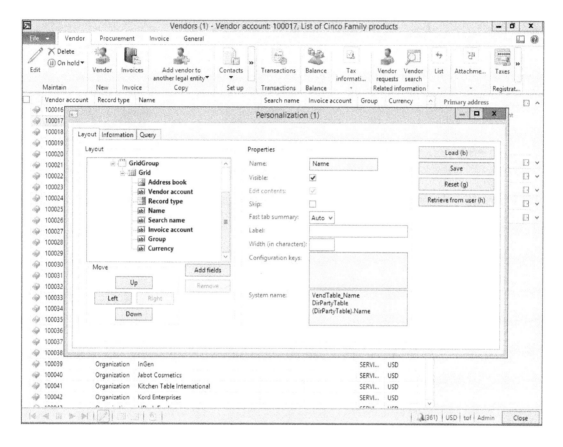

This will open up the **Personalization** dialog box and you can click on the **Add Fields** button.

Performing Bulk Updates Using The Edit In Grid Function

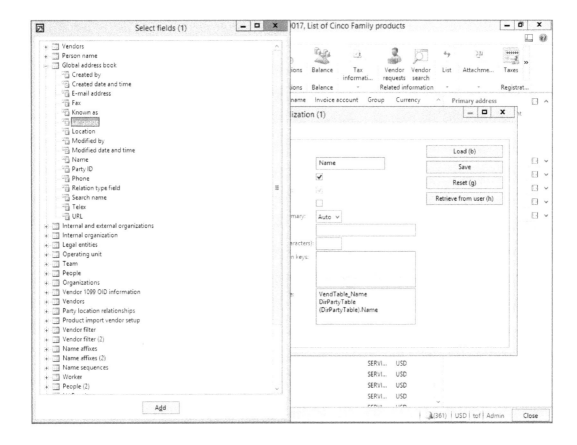

That will open up the field explorer and you can add any field from the related tables to the grid. For example, if you open up the **Global Address Book** group then you will be able to select the **Language** field and then click on the **Add** button to add it to the grid.

Performing Bulk Updates Using The Edit In Grid Function

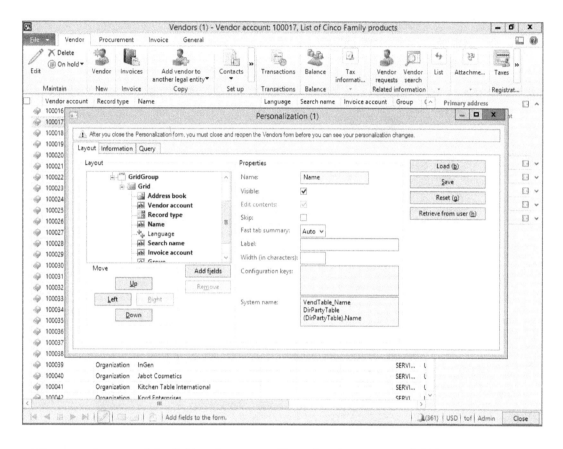

When you close out of the field explorer you will see that the **Language** field has been added to the grid. Then you can close the **Personalization** form.

Performing Bulk Updates Using The Edit In Grid Function

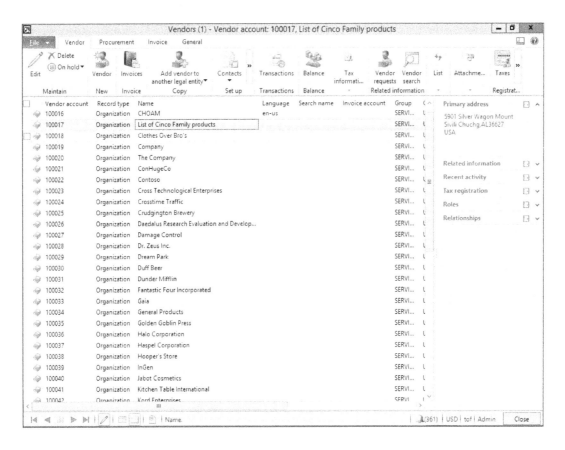

Now the grid will have the new fields that you added.

Performing Bulk Updates Using The Edit In Grid Function

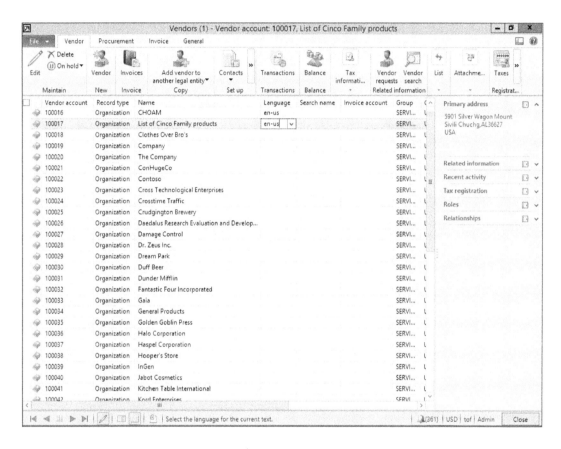

You can now just select the field and update it within the grid.

Performing Bulk Updates Using The Edit In Grid Function

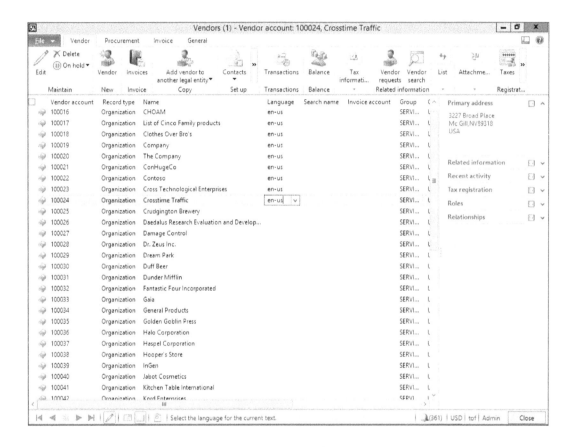

You can use the arrow keys to move through the records and update multiple fields.

That is too easy.

Performing Mass Updates Using Excel

Sometimes, if you have a lot of records to update you may want to use Excel as your maintenance tool.

Performing Mass Updates Using Excel

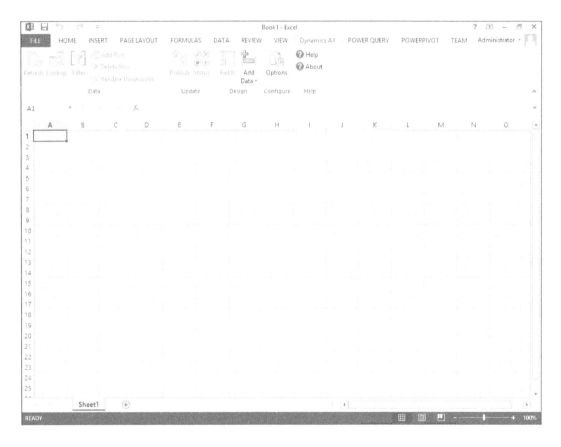

To do this, open up **Excel** and select the **Dynamics AX** ribbon bar.

Performing Mass Updates Using Excel

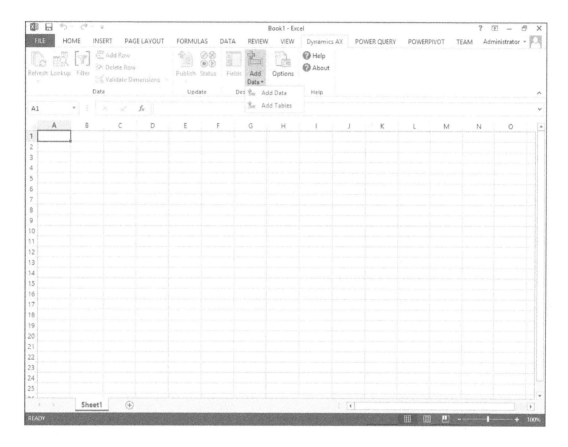

To get data from Dynamics AX, click on the **Add Data** button within the **Design** group of the **Dynamics AX** ribbon bar and then select the **Add Tables** menu item.

Performing Mass Updates Using Excel

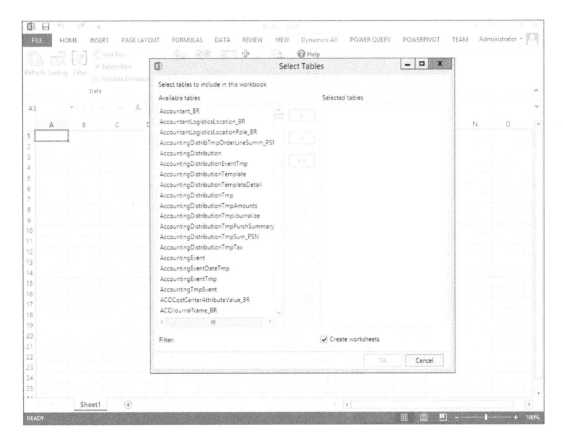

This will open up a **Select Tables** dialog box listing all of the tables within Dynamics AX.

Performing Mass Updates Using Excel

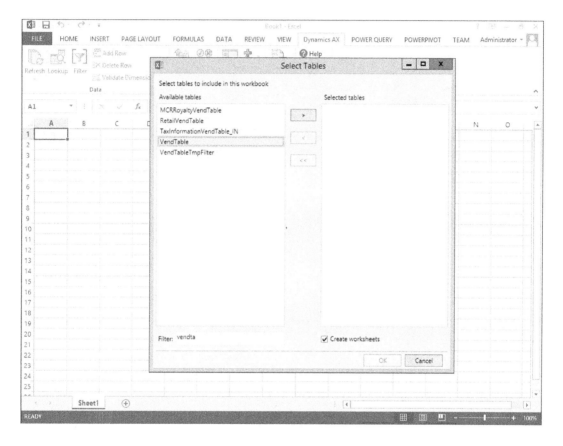

If you type in **VendTable** or any part of it within the **Filter** field then you will be able to select the **VendTable** table.

Performing Mass Updates Using Excel

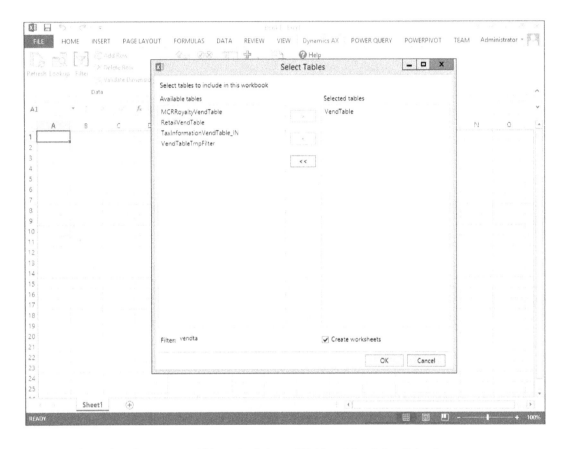

Then click on the **>** button to add it to the **Selected Tables** side of the dialog box.

When you have done that, click on the **OK** button.

Performing Mass Updates Using Excel

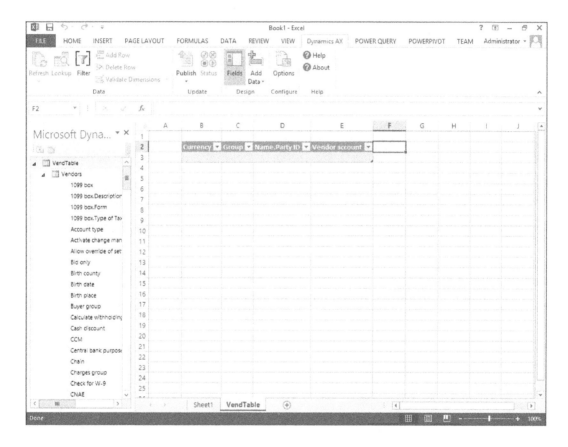

When you return back to Excel, you will have a field explorer on the left of the spreadsheet and some key fields from the table already loaded within the worksheet.

Performing Mass Updates Using Excel

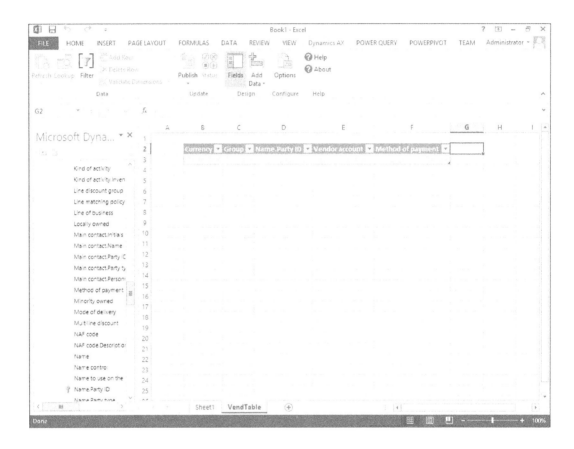

You can drag any fields from the field explorer over onto the worksheet.

Performing Mass Updates Using Excel

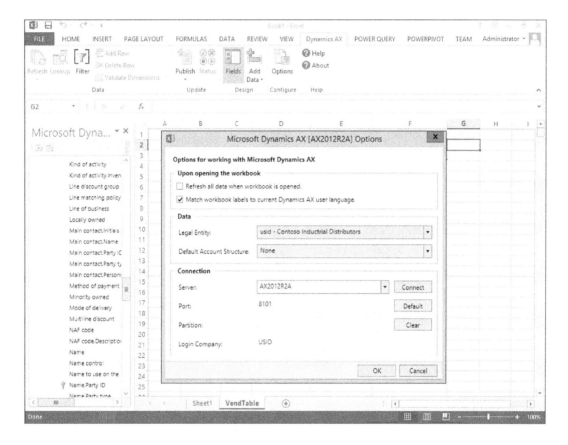

Before we start updating data though we need to make sure that we are connected to the right company within Dynamics AX. To do this, click on the **Options** button within the **Design** group of the **Dynamics AX** ribbon bar.

When the options form is displayed you will be able to see the company that you will be editing.

Performing Mass Updates Using Excel

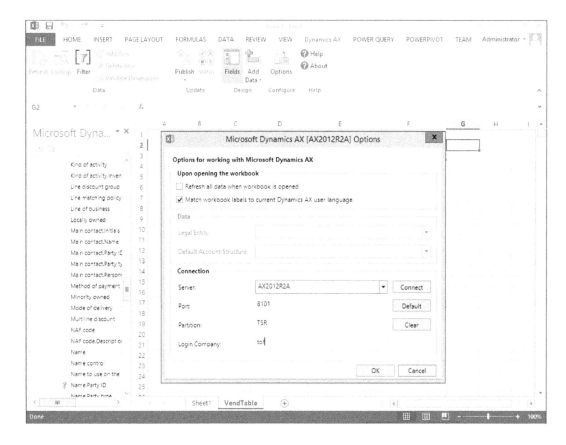

You can change the partition and also the login company and then click on the **Connect** button.

Performing Mass Updates Using Excel

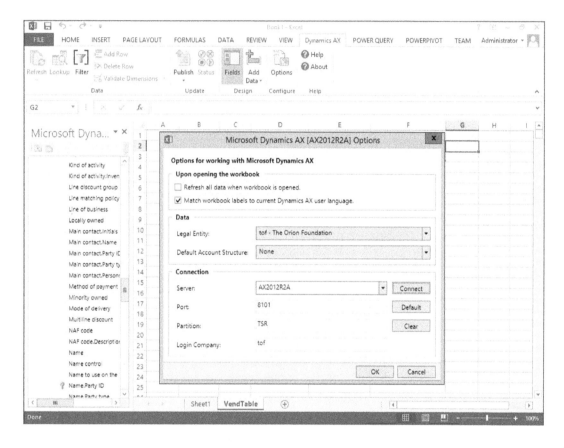

If everything works out for you then your Legal Entity will be updated and you can click on the **OK** button.

Performing Mass Updates Using Excel

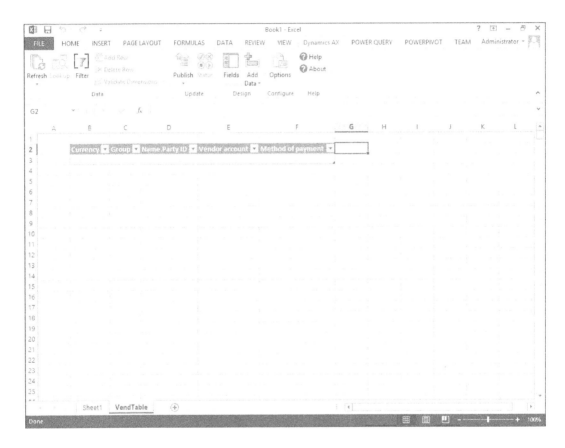

Now click on the **Fields** button to toggle out of the design mode and into edit mode.

Performing Mass Updates Using Excel

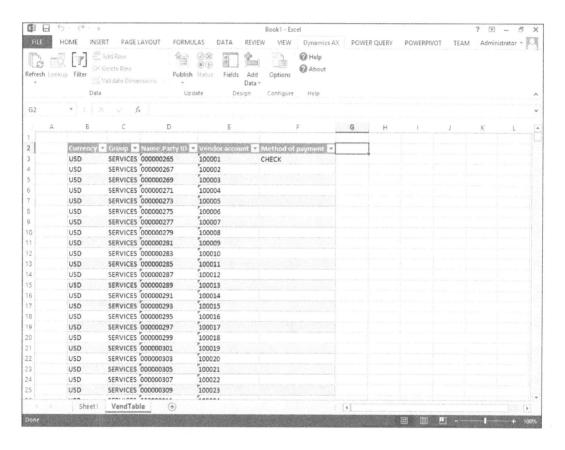

If you click on the **Refresh** button within the **Data** group of the **Dynamics AX** ribbon bar then Excel will go out and grab all of the records for you.

Performing Mass Updates Using Excel

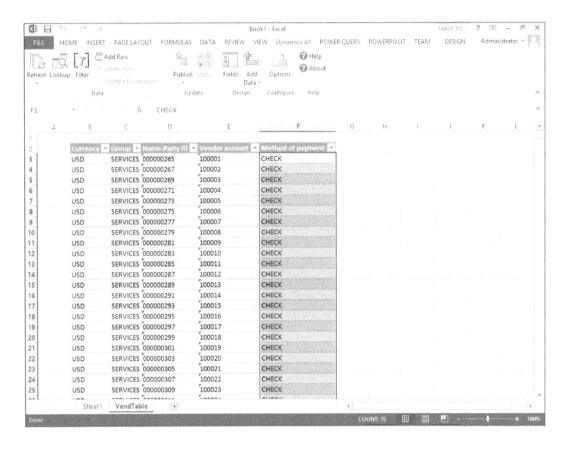

You can then perform mass updates within excel just like you would normally do.

Performing Mass Updates Using Excel

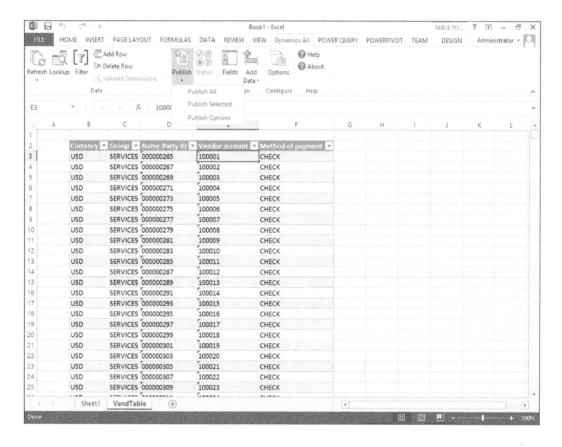

To update Dynamics AX, all you need to do is click on the **Publish** button within the **Update** group of the **Dynamics AX** ribbon bar and select the **Publish All** menu item.

Performing Mass Updates Using Excel

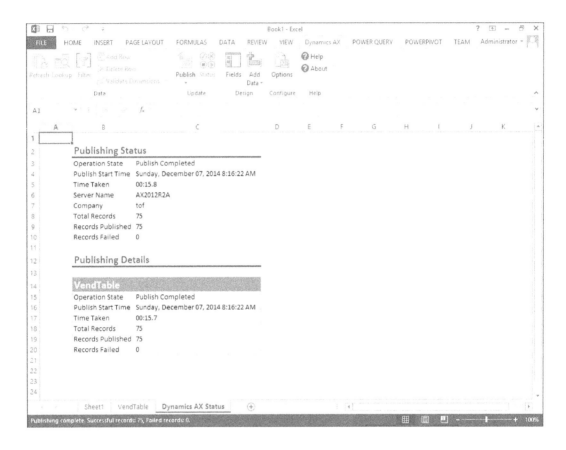

If all of the data that you updated is correct then you will be able to switch to the **Dynamics AX Status** worksheet and you will see how many records were updated.

Performing Mass Updates Using Excel

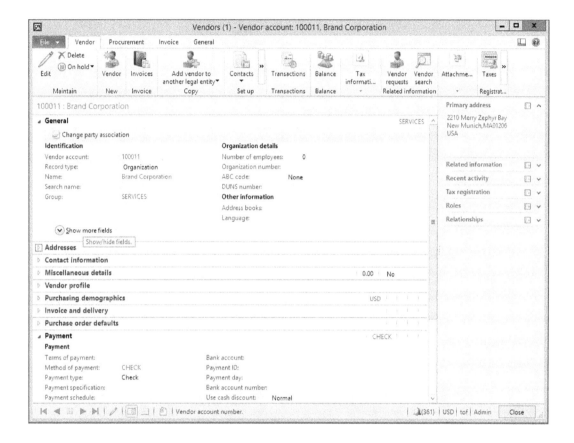

If you return back to your vendor details then you will see that the data was in fact updated.

That is too cool!

CONFIGURING INVOICING

Now that we have all of our vendors set up, we can start doing some real work by entering in invoices and processing payments.

Creating An Invoice Journal

The first step is to create an invoice journal and record it within the payables module.

Creating An Invoice Journal

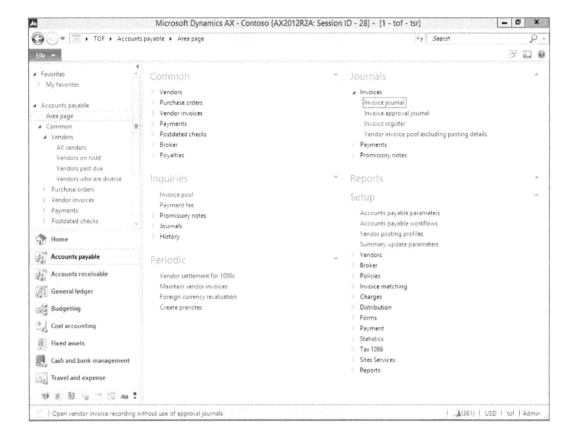

To do this, click on the **Invoice Journal** menu item within the **Invoices** folder of the **Journals** group within the **Accounts Payable** area page.

Creating An Invoice Journal

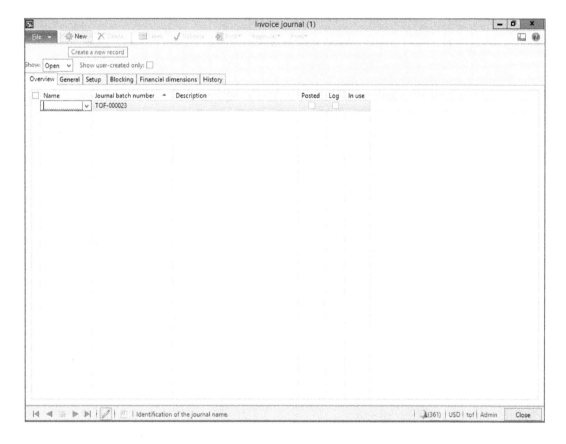

When the **Invoice Journal** list page is displayed, click on the **New** button within the menu bar to create a new record.

Creating An Invoice Journal

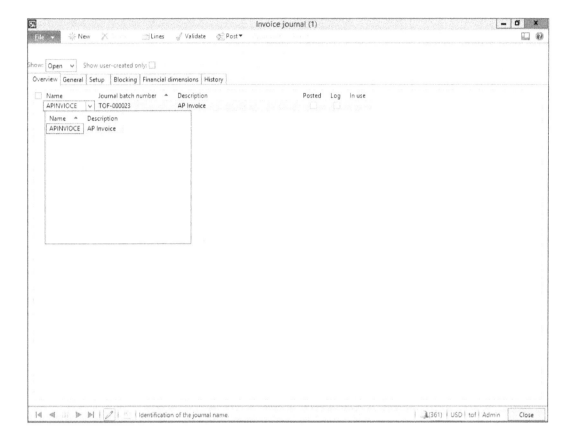

From the **Name** dropdown list, select the **APINVOICE** journal option.

Creating An Invoice Journal

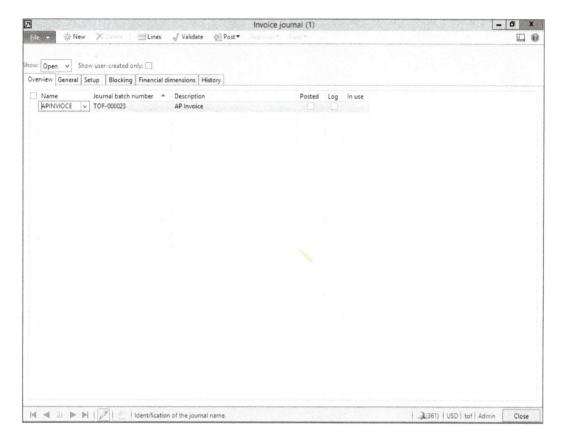

Once you have done that, click on the **Lines** button in the menu bar to start entering in the line detail.

Creating An Invoice Journal

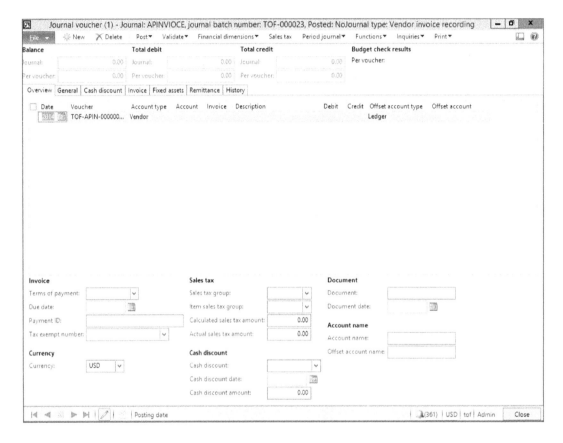

When the **Journal Voucher** maintenance form is displayed, click on the **New** button in the menu bar to create a new voucher line.

Creating An Invoice Journal

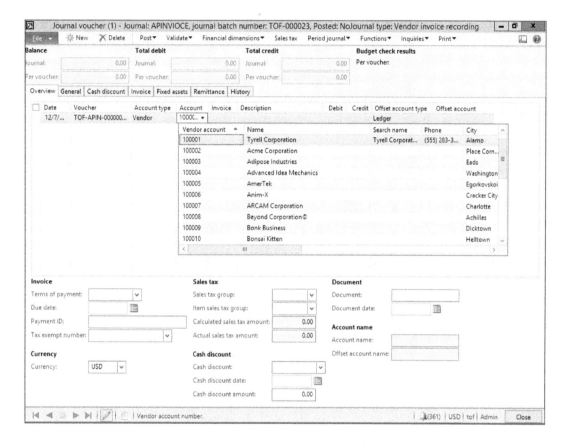

Click on the **Account** dropdown list and select the vendor that you want to create the invoice journal line for.

Creating An Invoice Journal

Then enter in an **Invoice** number for reference.

Creating An Invoice Journal

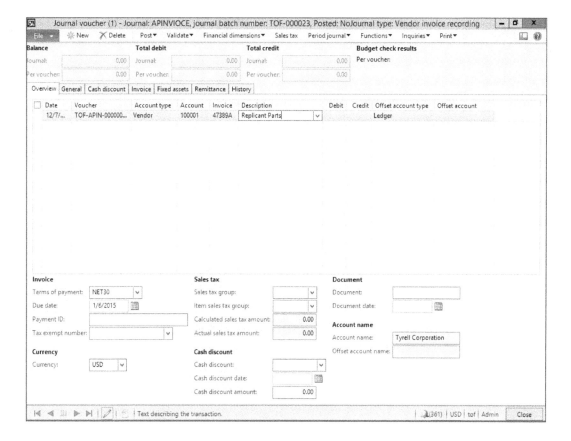

And you can also add more detail by entering in a **Description**.

Creating An Invoice Journal

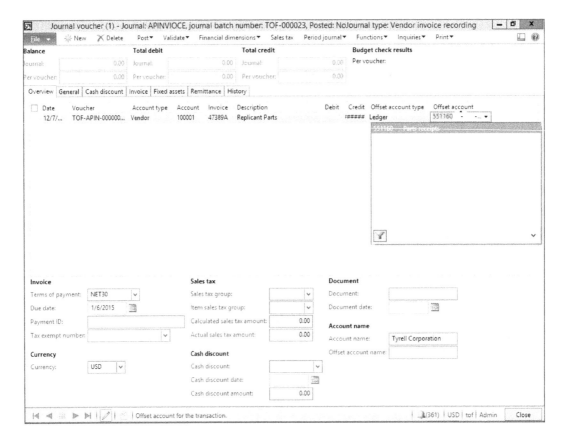

Enter in the **Credit** amount for the invoice and then from the **Offset Account** dropdown list and select the main account that you want to offset the invoice against.

Creating An Invoice Journal

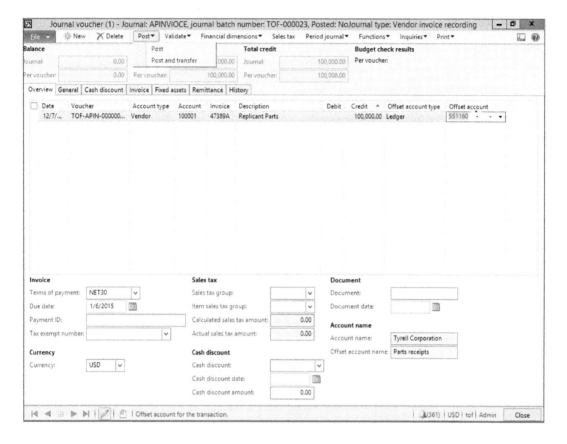

You can continue adding additional invoice lines within the journal if you like, and when you are done, click on the **Post** button within the menu bar and select the **Post** menu item.

Creating An Invoice Journal

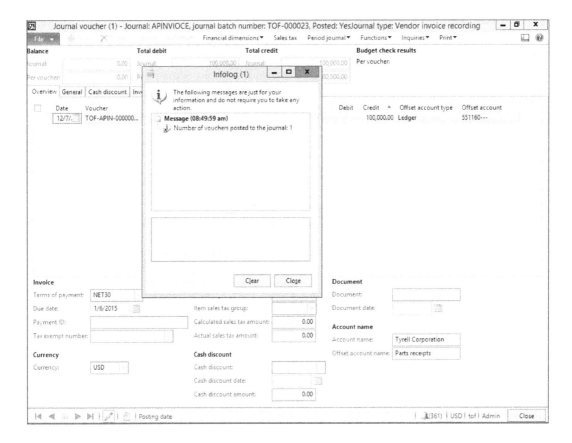

This will update your invoice journal for you and you should get an InfoLog message.

Creating An Invoice Journal

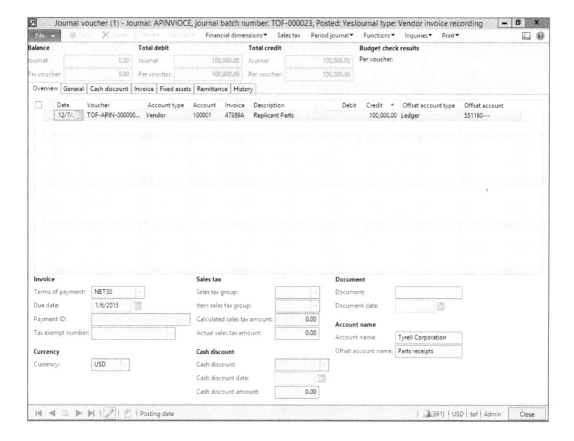

Once the journal has been posted, click on the **Close** button to exit from the form.

Creating An Invoice Journal

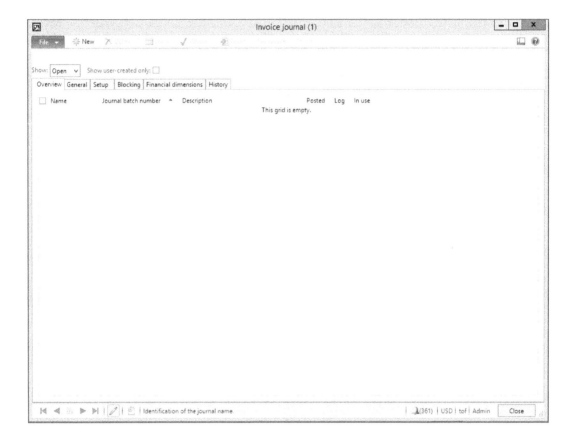

You may notice that when you return to the **Invoice Journal** list page you don't see any journal entries. That is because by default it is only showing you the open journals.

Creating An Invoice Journal

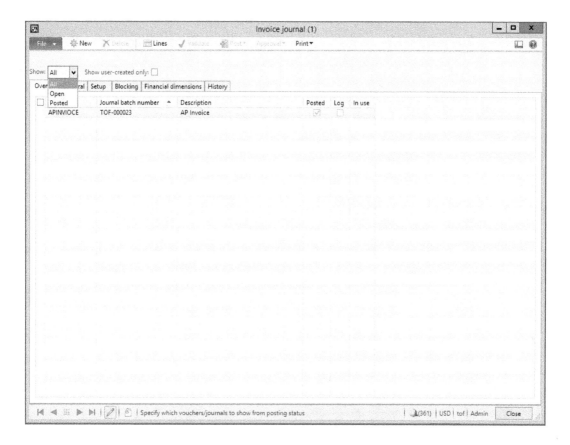

If you click on the dropdown list for the **Show** field in the form header then you can select the **All** option and you will be able to see all of the journals, including the ones that have been posted.

Viewing All Open Vendor Invoices

Once you have created your payables invoice journals you can visit them any time you like to review them.

Viewing All Open Vendor Invoices

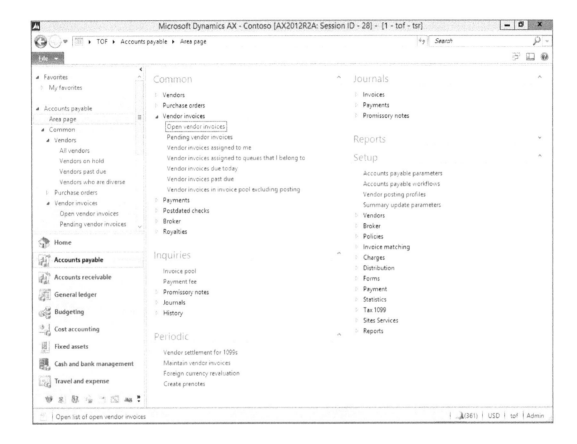

To do this, click on the **Open Vendor Invoices** menu item within the **Vendor Invoices** folder of the **Common** group of the **Accounts Payable** area page.

Viewing All Open Vendor Invoices

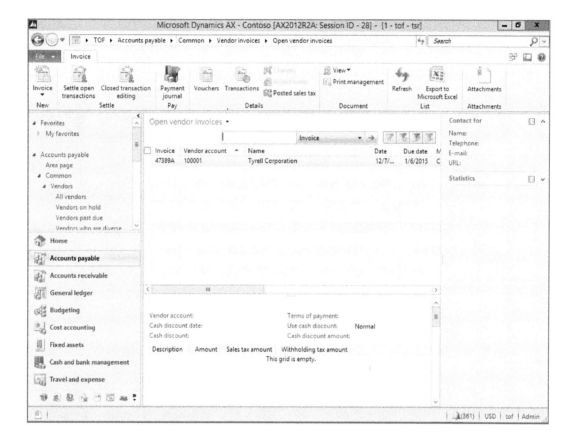

This will open up a list page showing you all of the outstanding payables invoices.

Viewing All Open Vendor Invoices

If you double click on any of them you will be able to drill down into the invoice details – in this case it's the invoice journal that we just created.

CREATING VENDOR PAYMENTS

Once you have invoices within the system, you can start selecting invoices for payment and print checks.

Creating A Payment Journal Using Payment Proposals

To start the process all we need to do is create a payment journal and select the invoices that we want to pay.

Creating A Payment Journal Using Payment Proposals

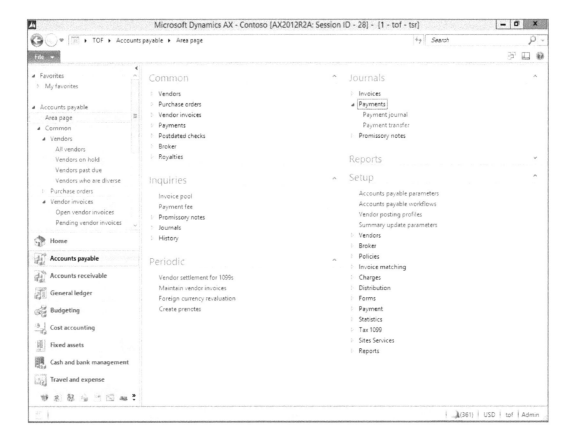

To do this click on the **Payment Journal** menu item within the **Payments** folder of the **Journals** group within the **Accounts Payable** area page.

Creating A Payment Journal Using Payment Proposals

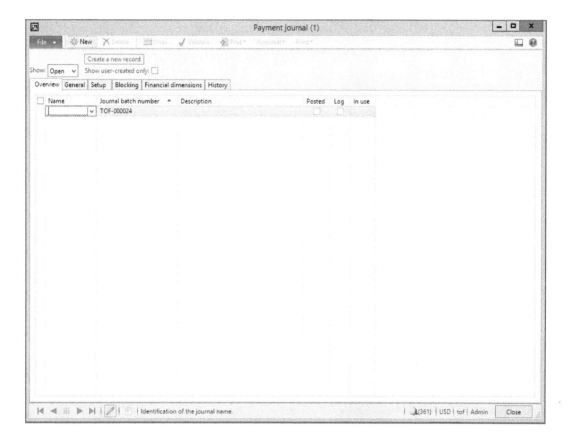

When the **Payment Journal** list page is displayed, click on the **New** button to create a new payment journal record.

Creating A Payment Journal Using Payment Proposals

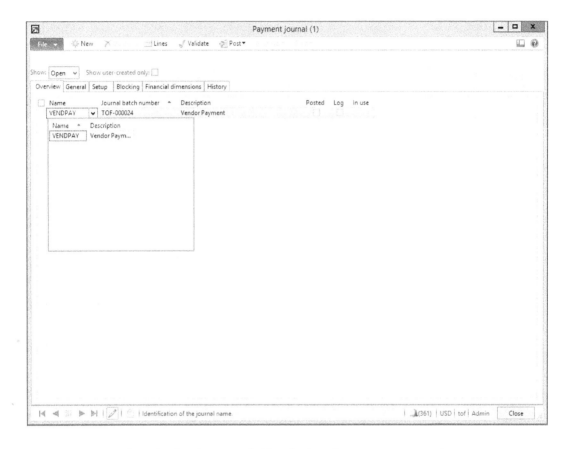

Click on the dropdown list for the **Name** field and select the **VENDPAY** journal type.

Creating A Payment Journal Using Payment Proposals

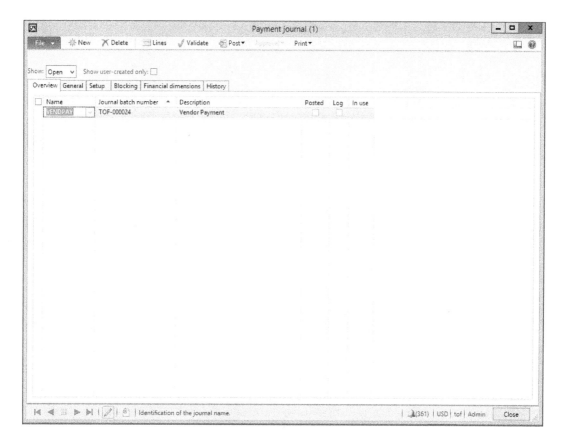

After creating the payment journal header, click on the **Lines** button in the menu bar.

Creating A Payment Journal Using Payment Proposals

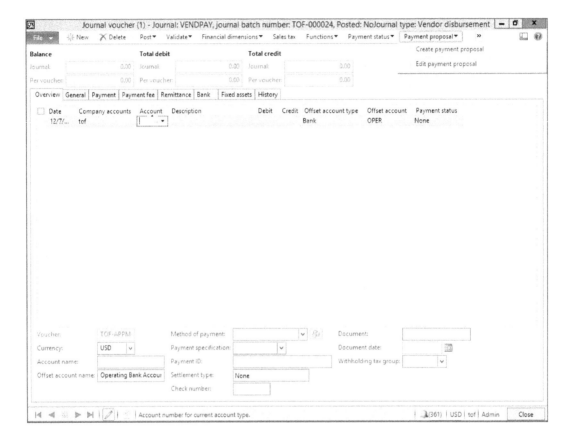

This will take you to the Payment **Journal Voucher** maintenance form.

Although you can enter in all of the payment details one at a time, a better way is to use the payment proposal tool to select the invoices to pay for you. To do this, click on the **Payment Proposal** button within the menu bar and click on the **Create Payment Proposal** menu item.

Creating A Payment Journal Using Payment Proposals

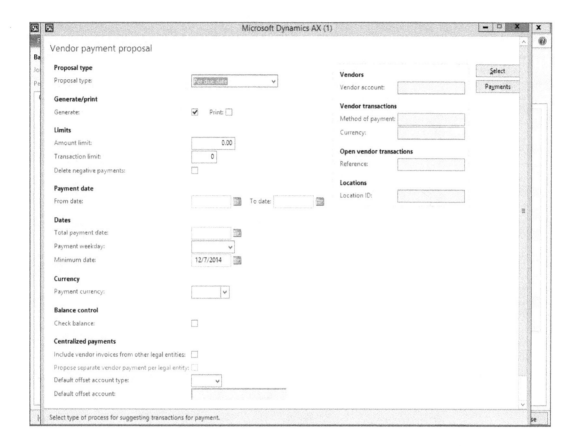

This will open up the **Vendor Payment Proposal** selection screen. To select all of the outstanding invoices leave the defaults as they are, and click on the **OK** button at the bottom of the form.

Creating A Payment Journal Using Payment Proposals

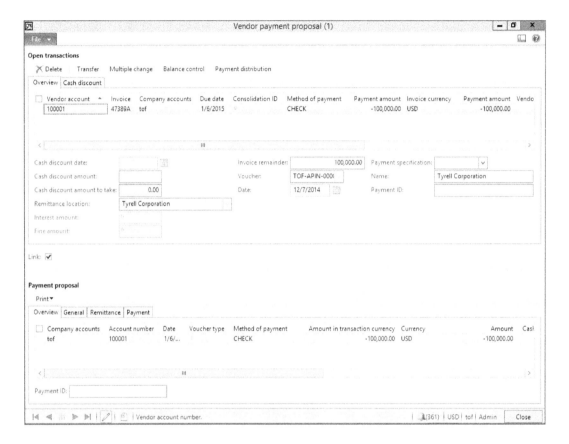

This will open up a form with all of the outstanding payables invoices that need to be paid.

Creating A Payment Journal Using Payment Proposals

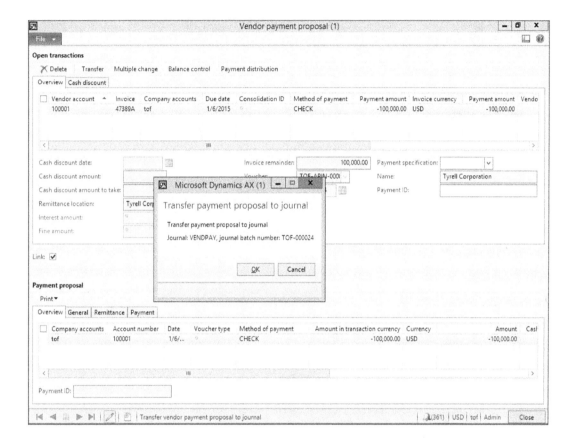

To select them all, just click on the **Transfer** button in the menu bar and when the dialog box is displayed, click on the **OK** button to confirm the transfer of the lines to the payment journal.

Creating A Payment Journal Using Payment Proposals

When you return to the payment journal you will see that the invoice details have been populated for you.

Generating Payments From A Payment Journal

Once you have selected the invoices that you want to pay, you can start generating the payments.

Generating Payments From A Payment Journal

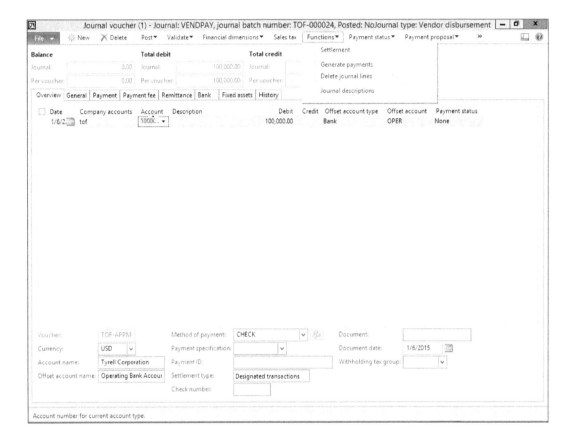

To do this, click on the **Functions** menu item within the menu bar of the **Payment Journal Voucher** maintenance form, and select the **Generate Payments** menu item.

Generating Payments From A Payment Journal

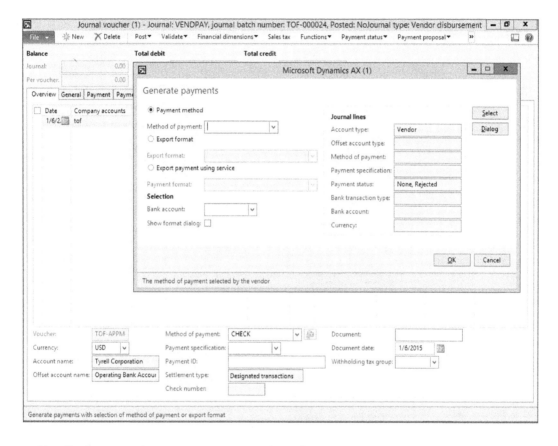

This will take you to the **Generate Payments** dialog form.

Generating Payments From A Payment Journal

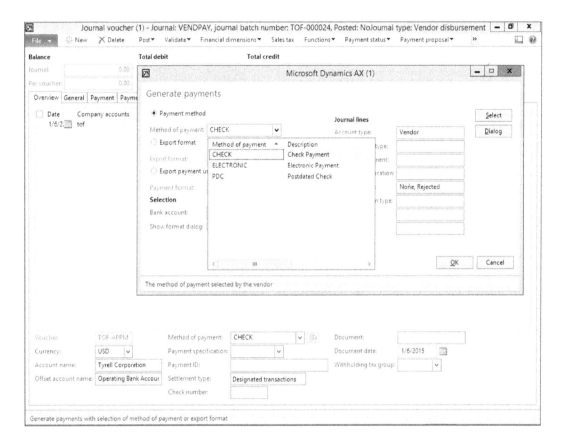

Click on the **Method Of Payment** dropdown list and select the **CHECK** option.

Generating Payments From A Payment Journal

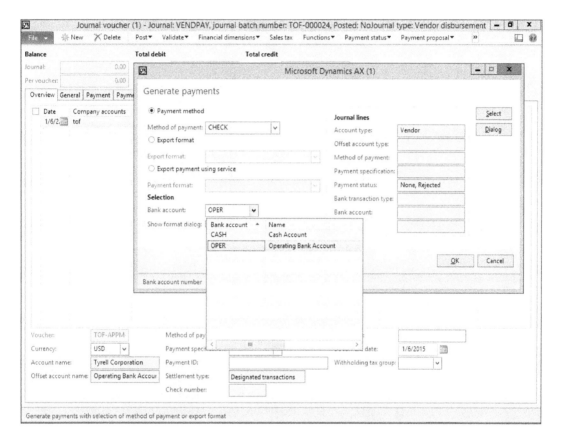

Then click on the **Bank Account** dropdown list and select the bank that you want to create the disbursement from.

Generating Payments From A Payment Journal

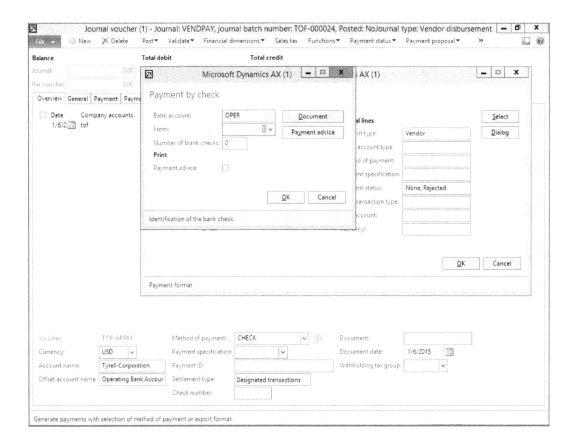

If you click the **OK** button at this point then the checks will be generated and sent directly to the printer. If you want to see the checks themselves on screen then click on the **Dialog** button and then when the **Payment By Check** dialog box is displayed, click on the **Payment Advice** button.

Generating Payments From A Payment Journal

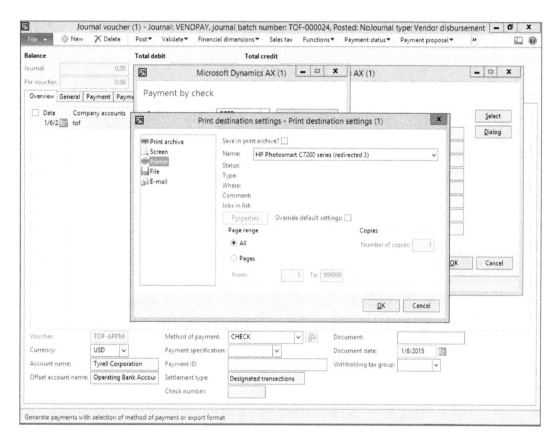

This will open up the **Print Destination Settings** dialog box.

Generating Payments From A Payment Journal

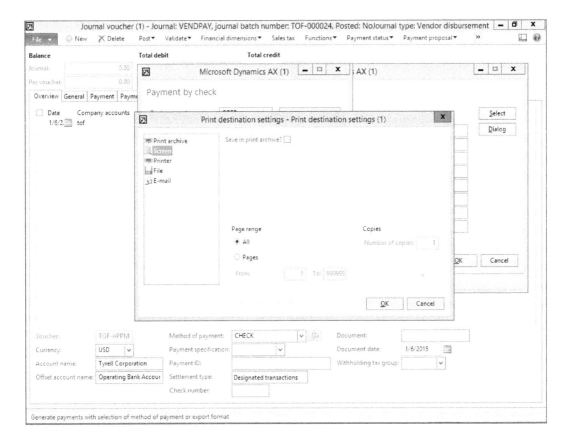

You can change the destination from **Printer** to **Screen** top tell the system to print the check and then show it to you.

When you have done that just click on the **OK** button and save your preferences.

Generating Payments From A Payment Journal

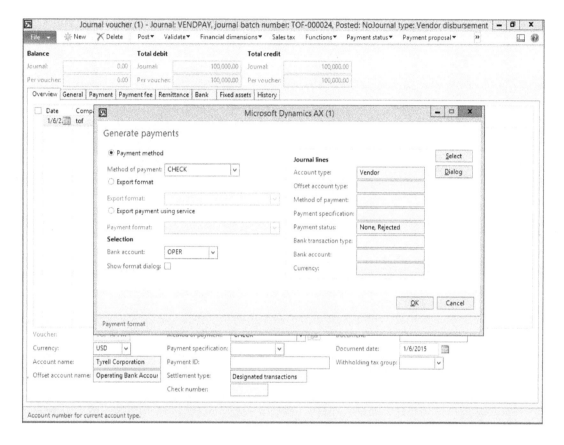

When you return back to the **Generate Payments** dialog box click on the **OK** button.

Generating Payments From A Payment Journal

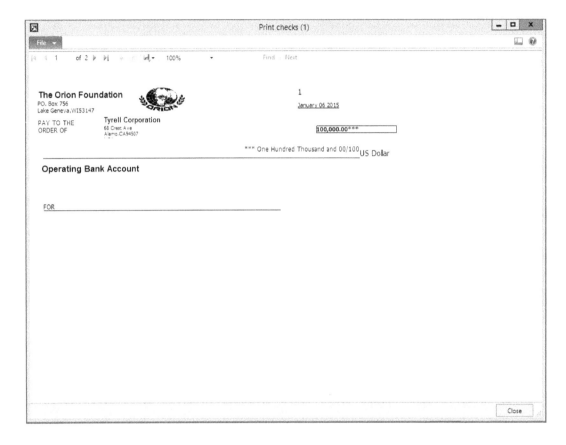

The next thing that you should see is a check.

Generating Payments From A Payment Journal

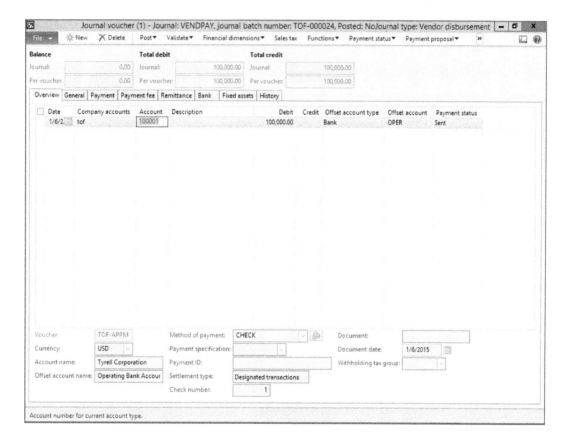

When you close out of the check you will notice that the payment line will now have a check number associated with it.

Generating Payments From A Payment Journal

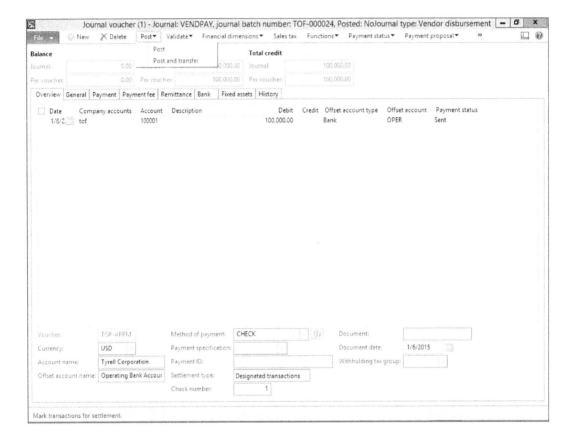

All that is left to do now is to click on the **Post** button in the menu bar and click on the **Post** menu item.

Generating Payments From A Payment Journal

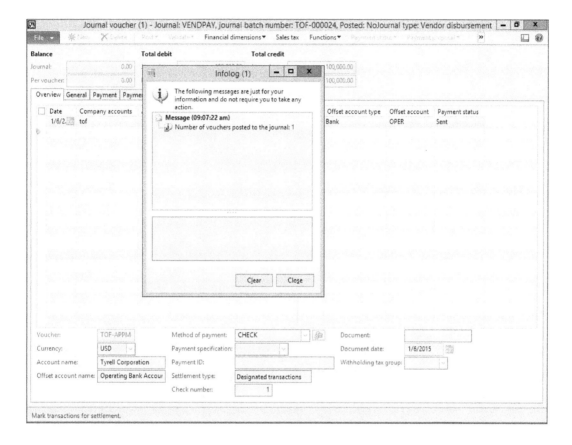

That will post your journal for you and you can close out of the payment journal.

Generating Payments From A Payment Journal

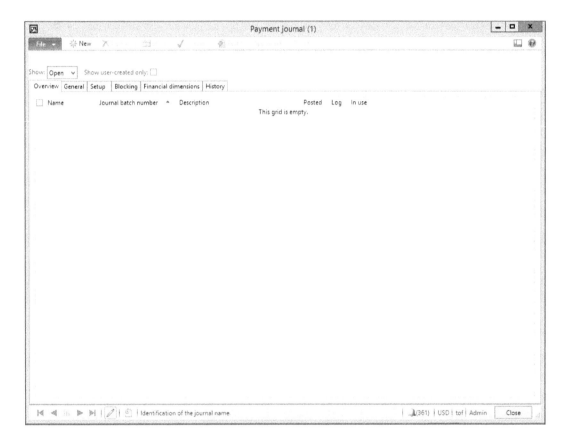

As with the other journal, you will notice that the payment journal disappears from the Payment Journals list page.

Generating Payments From A Payment Journal

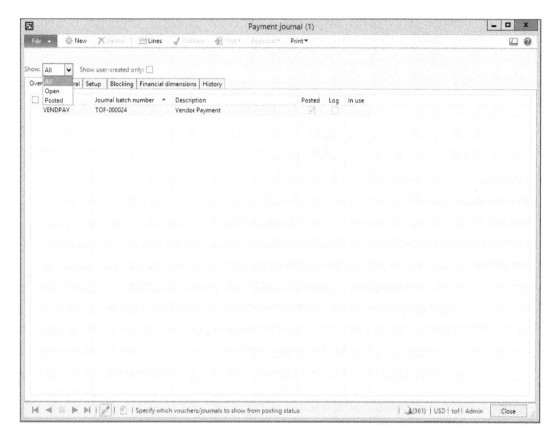

But if you change the **Show** option to **All** then you will be able to see all of the posted payments.

Viewing Vendor Transaction History

Now that you have transactions posted against your vendors you can see all of the detail directly from the vendor itself.

Viewing Vendor Transaction History

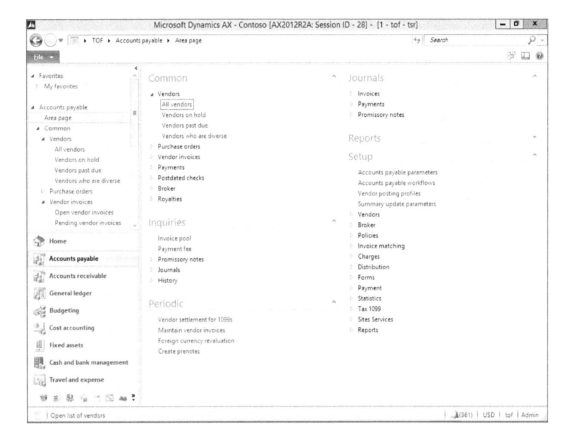

To see this, click on the **All Vendors** menu item within the **Vendors** folder of the **Common** group within the **Accounts Payable** area page.

Viewing Vendor Transaction History

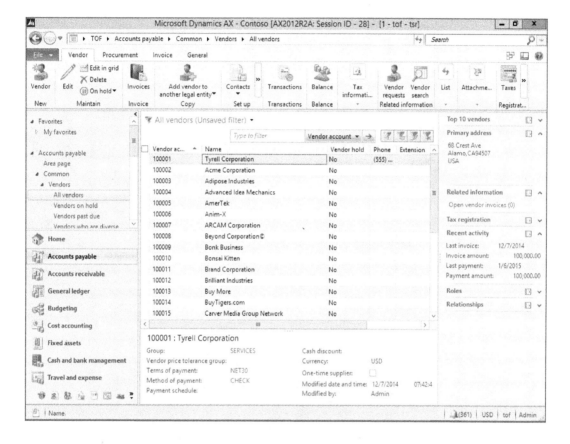

When the **All Vendors** list page is displayed, double click on the vendor that you want to inquire on.

Viewing Vendor Transaction History

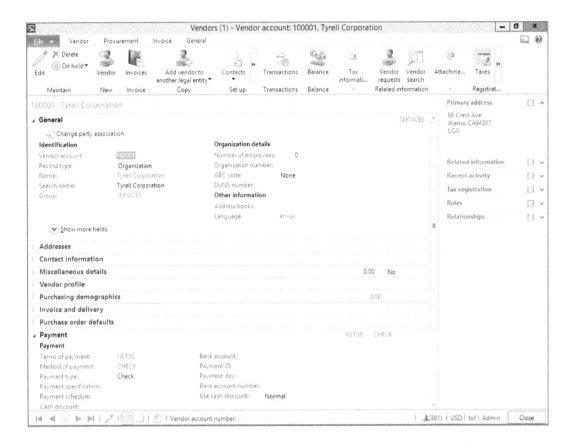

When the vendor details are shown, to view all of the journals, just click on the **Transactions** button within the **Transactions** group of the **Vendor** ribbon bar.

Viewing Vendor Transaction History

This will open up the **Vendor Transactions** list page and you will be able to see all of the history for the vendor.

Viewing Vendor Transaction History

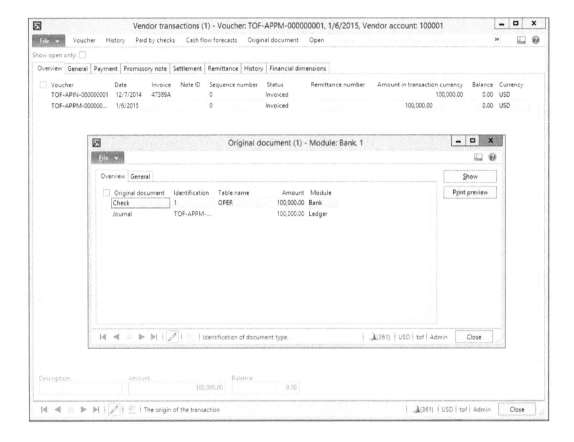

If you click on the **Original Document** button in the menu bar you will also be able to see the original transactions. If you want to view a copy of the check, just select the check line an then click on the **Print Preview** button.

Viewing Vendor Transaction History

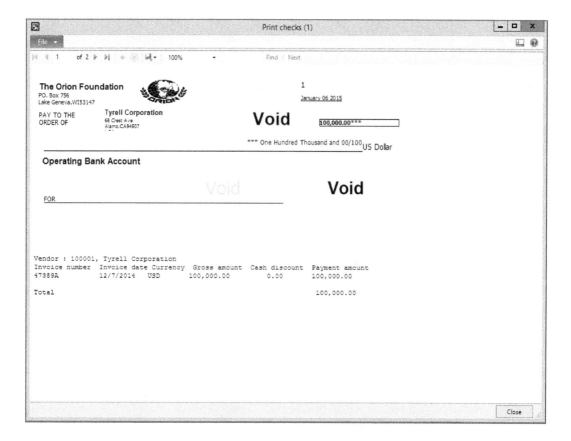

You will then see a voided copy of the original check transaction.

How easy is that?

CONFIGURING PAYABLES INVOICE JOURNAL APPROVALS

Payables is one of the most common areas within Finance that people want to add workflows and a great place to start within this module is to configure workflow approvals around the Payables Invoice Journals so that you can make sure that only the invoices that you want to pay get paid.

Creating An Invoice Journal Workflow

The first step is to create a workflow that we can then attach to our Payables Invoice Journals.

Creating An Invoice Journal Workflow

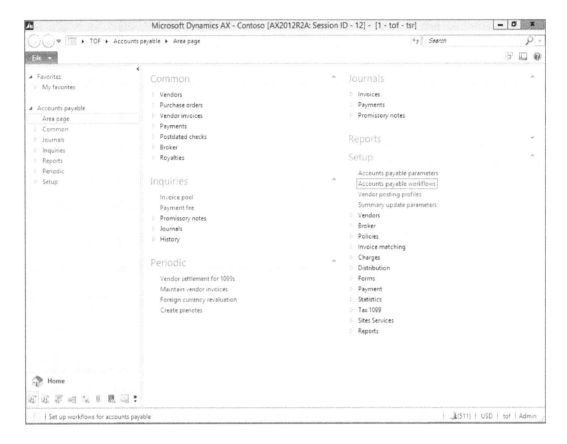

Start off by clicking on the **Accounts Payable Workflows** menu item within the **Setup** group of the **Accounts Payable** area page.

Creating An Invoice Journal Workflow

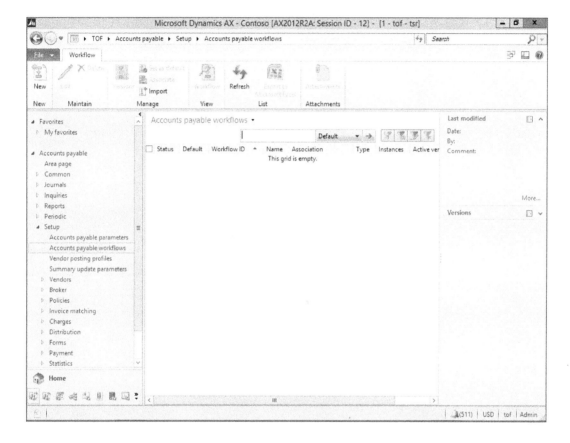

When the **Accounts Payable Workflow** list page is displayed, click on the **New** button within the **New** group of the **Workflow** ribbon bar.

Creating An Invoice Journal Workflow

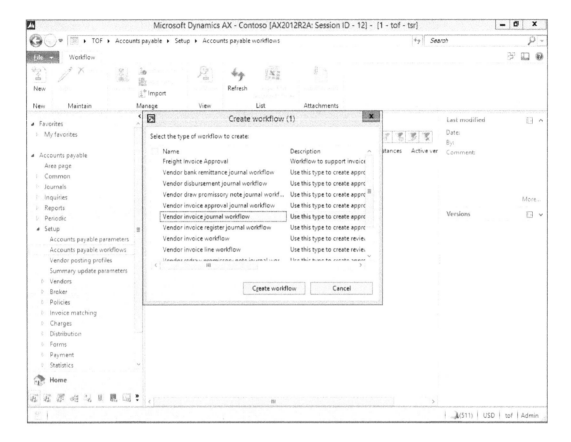

When the **Create Workflow** dialog box is displayed with all of the available workflow templates listed, select the **Vendor Invoice Journal Workflow** template, and then click the **Create Workflow** button.

Creating An Invoice Journal Workflow

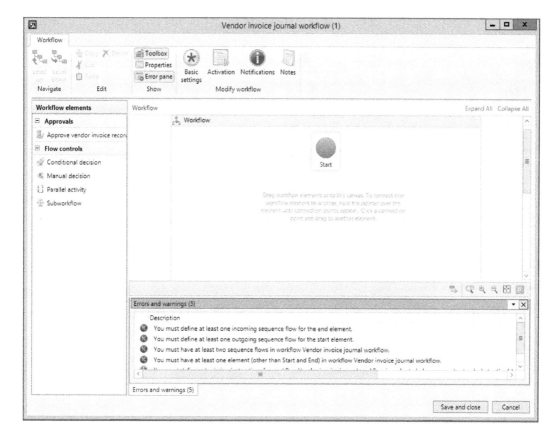

Dynamics AX will then open up the new workflow template showing you the workflow designer canvas.

Creating An Invoice Journal Workflow

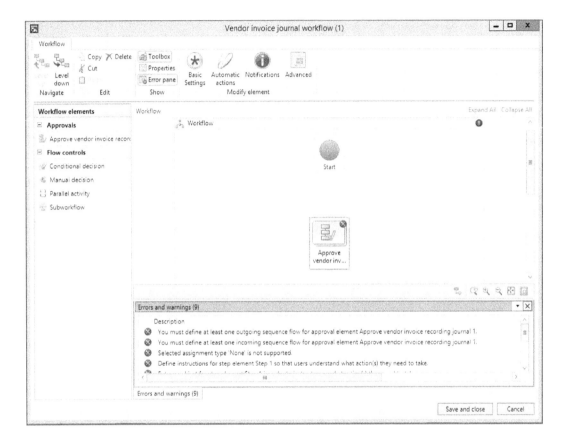

Drag the **Approve Vendor Invoice Record** workflow element from the palette on the left hand side of the designer onto the workflow canvas/

Creating An Invoice Journal Workflow

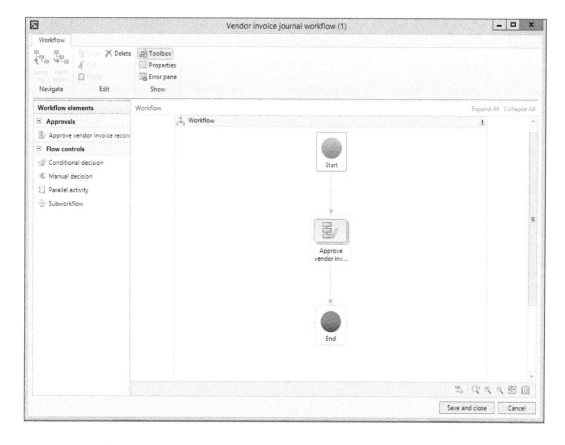

Then link the **Start** element to the **Approve** task, and then link the **Approve** task to the **End** element so that the workflow has a valid path.

Defining Invoice Journal Approval Workflow Submission Instructions

Once you have the workflow correctly linked, you will want to start tidying it up and tying up the loose ends on the workflow. The first task is to configure the **Submission Instructions** so that the user knows what they are submitting the invoice document for.

Defining Invoice Journal Approval Workflow Submission Instructions

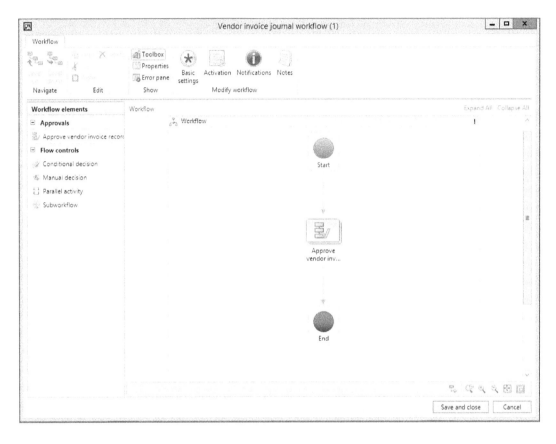

To do this, select the **Workflow** frame that bounds the workflow elements, and then click on the **Basic Settings** button within the **Modify Workflow** group of the **Workflow** ribbon bar.

Defining Invoice Journal Approval Workflow Submission Instructions

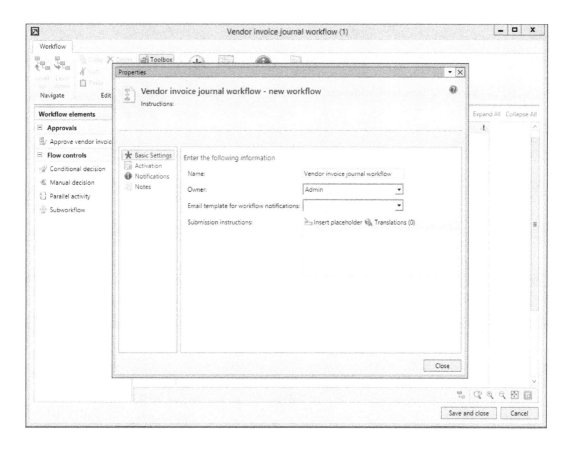

When the **Properties** maintenance form is displayed, it should automatically be showing the **Basic Settings Page** and you can give your workflow a **Name** to better describe it.

Note: This is important if you have multiple versions of the workflow, because you can easily differentiate them when they display in a list.

Defining Invoice Journal Approval Workflow Submission Instructions

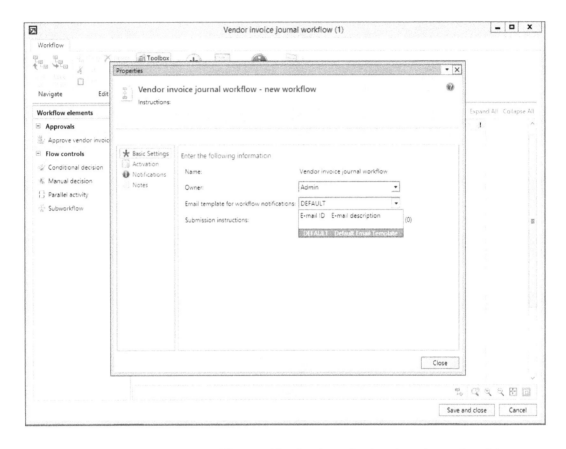

Select the **Email Template For Workflow Notification** from the dropdown list so that if the notification is sent via e-mail then you have a template that it is able to use.

Defining Invoice Journal Approval Workflow Submission Instructions

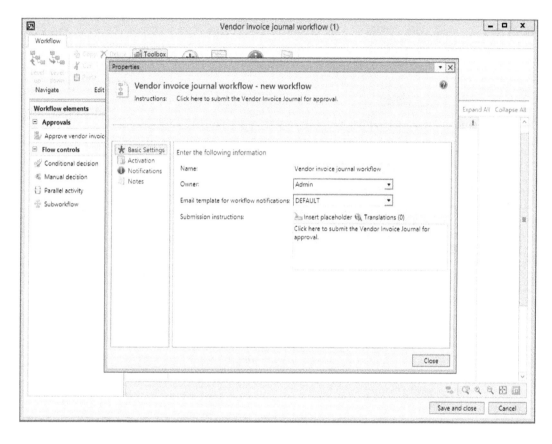

Then add some **Submission Instructions** which will allow the user to see what they are getting themselves into when they start the submission process.

Assigning Multiple People To The Journal Approval Workflow Task

Workflows do not have to be sent to just one person. If multiple people are able to approve workflows then you can add them all to the workflow steps. This also has the added benefit that you can define how many of the people need to approve the task before it continues on. You can tell the system that one, all, the majority, or a percentage of the users reed to respond, giving you a lot of flexibility around the approval process.

Assigning Multiple People To The Journal Approval Workflow Task

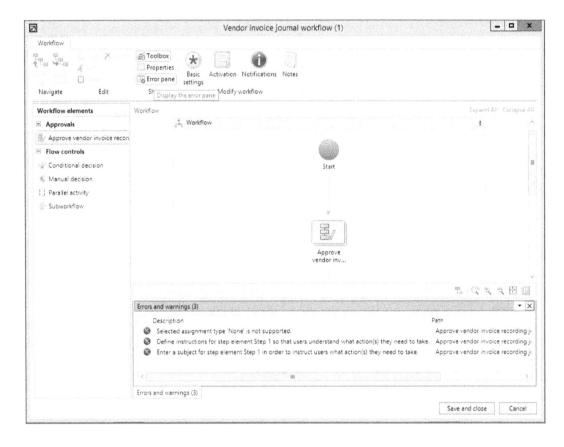

If the **Errors and Warnings** panel is not shown, click on the **Error Pane** button within the **Show** group of the **Workflow** ribbon bar. Then double click on the error message that says that the **Selected assignment type "None" is not supported.**

Assigning Multiple People To The Journal Approval Workflow Task

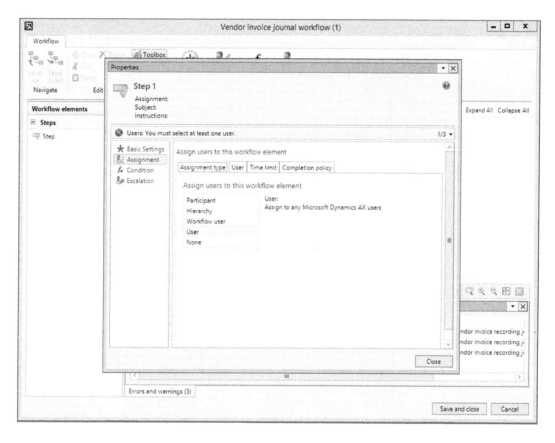

This will take you straight to the **Properties** maintenance form and show you the **Assignment** page. Select the **User** assignment type from the list of option.

Assigning Multiple People To The Journal Approval Workflow Task

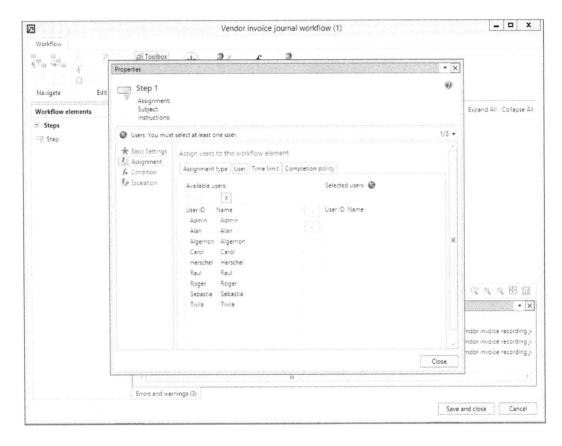

Switch to the **User** tab, and then select all of the users that you want to participate in this approval task from the list of **Available Users**.

Assigning Multiple People To The Journal Approval Workflow Task

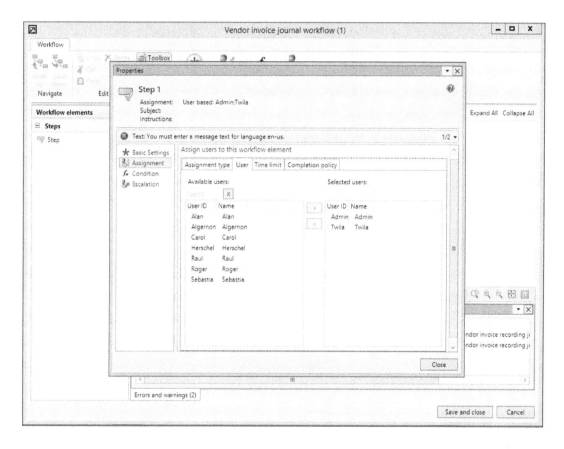

Then click on the **>** button to move them to the **Selected Users** list.

Assigning Multiple People To The Journal Approval Workflow Task

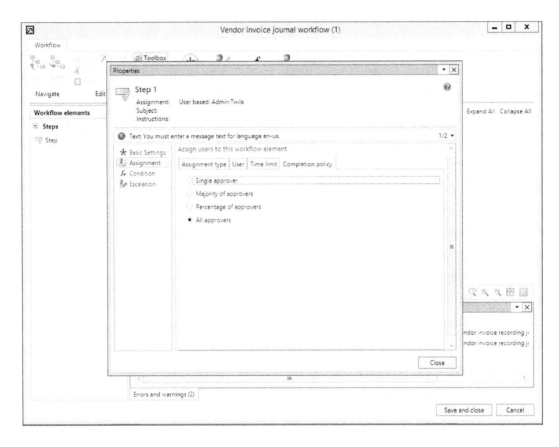

Now change to the **Completion Policy** tab. By default the **All approvers** option is selected indicating that all of the selected users will have to approve the task becore it will move to the next step.

Assigning Multiple People To The Journal Approval Workflow Task

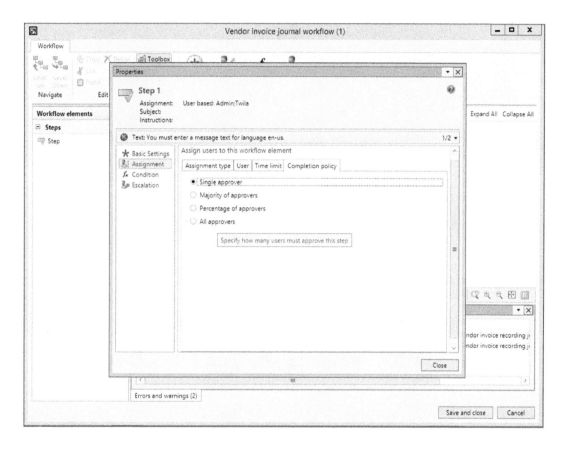

To make this a quicker workflow process, select the **Single Approver** option so that just one of the selected workers needs to approve the task for it to be approved.

When you are finished, click on the **Close** button to exit from the form.

Defining The Journal Approval Workflow Task Instructions With Context Links

Additionally we want to configure the workflow task instructions so that when the tasks are assigned to the users that they understand what they are being asked to do.

Defining The Journal Approval Workflow Task Instructions With Context Links

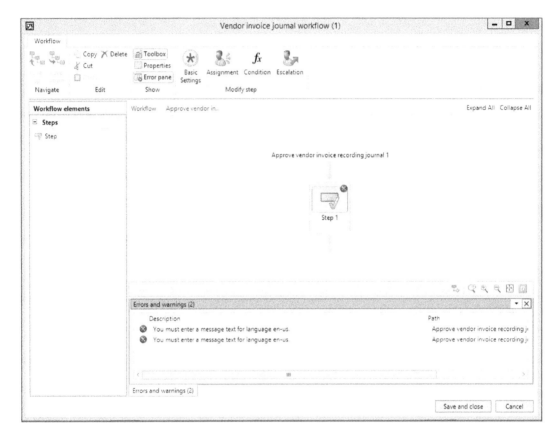

To do this either click on one of the remaining messages within the **Error** panel, or select the **Step 1** workflow element that is below the **Approve Invoice** workflow element and then click on the **Basic Settings** button within the **Modify Step** group of the **Workflow** ribbon bar.

Defining The Journal Approval Workflow Task Instructions With Context Links

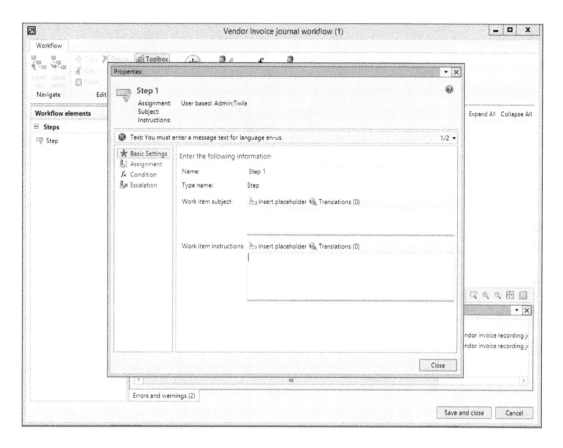

This will open up the **Properties** for the workflow task.

Defining The Journal Approval Workflow Task Instructions With Context Links

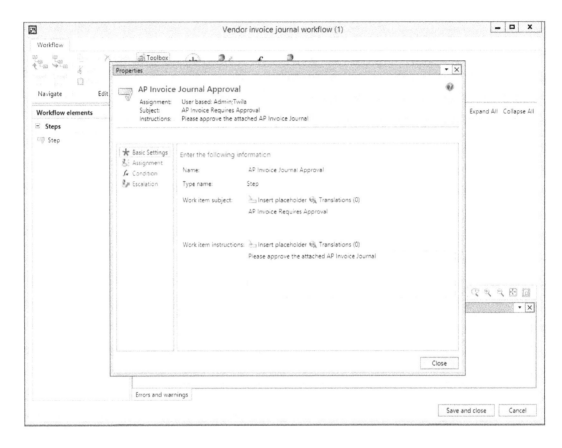

Assign your task a more descriptive **Name**, then update the **Work Item Subject** which will be the message in the header of the message sent to the user, and also add some **Work Item Instructions** to describe to the user what they are expected to do as part of the task.

Defining The Journal Approval Workflow Task Instructions With Context Links

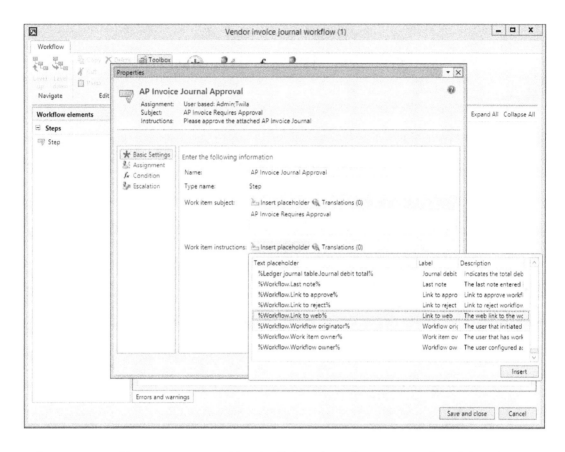

If you want to add some context sensitive details into the task instructions then click on the **Insert Placeholder** button and you will see a list of all the available text placeholders that you can embed in your messages. If you scroll down to the bottom of the list you will be able to select the **%Workflow.Link To Web%** placeholder which will add a URL that will take the user directly to the workflow task through the portals.

Defining The Journal Approval Workflow Task Instructions With Context Links

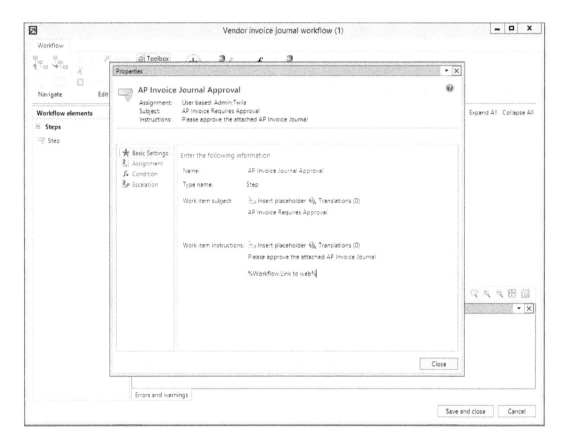

After you have updated the instructions then you can click on the **Close** button and exit from the form.

Publishing And Activating The Journal Approval Workflow

Once the workflow has been defined, and all of the errors and messages have been resolved, all that is left to di is to publish and activate the workflow.

Publishing And Activating The Journal Approval Workflow

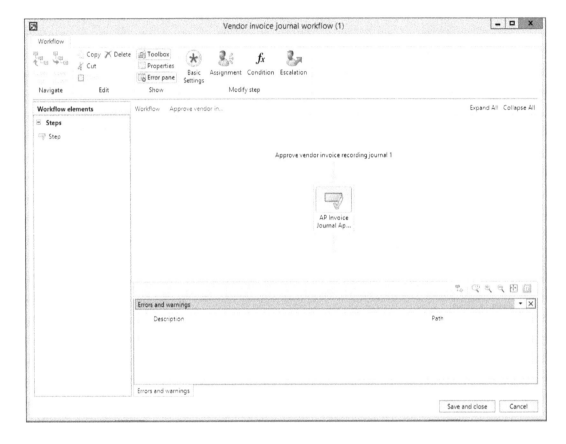

To do this, click on the **Save And Close** button at the bottom right of the workflow designer.

Publishing And Activating The Journal Approval Workflow

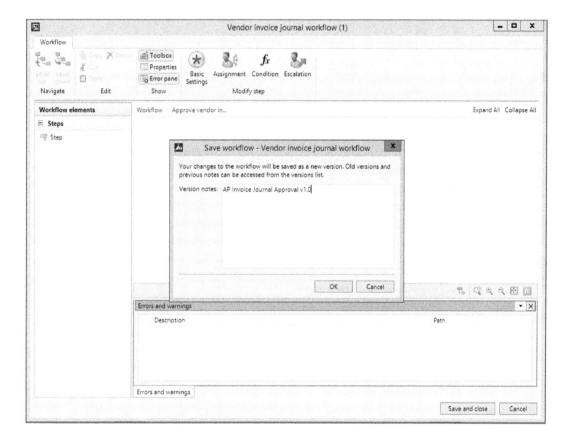

When the **Version Notes** dialog box is displayed, you can add comments about the workflow version, and then click the **OK** button.

Publishing And Activating The Journal Approval Workflow

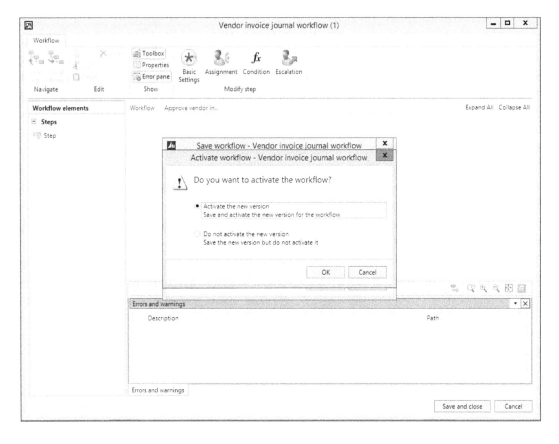

When the **Activate Workflow** dialog box is displayed, select the **Activate The New Version** option and then click the **OK** button.

Publishing And Activating The Journal Approval Workflow

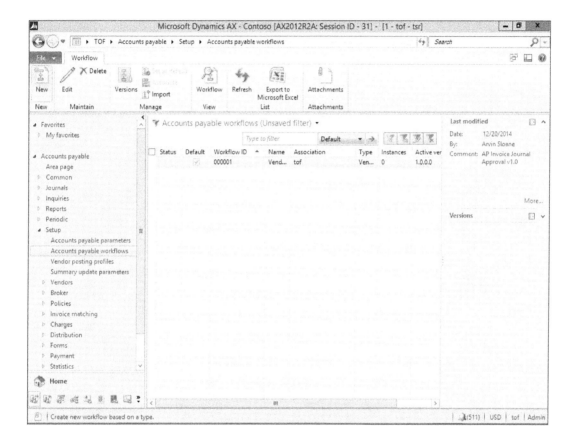

Now when you return to the **Accounts Payable Workflow** list page, you should see your new workflow.

Assign The Invoice Journal Workflow To The Invoice Journal

All that remains to be done now is to link the workflow to your **Payables Invoice Journal** so that it will be managed through the workflow process.

Assign The Invoice Journal Workflow To The Invoice Journal

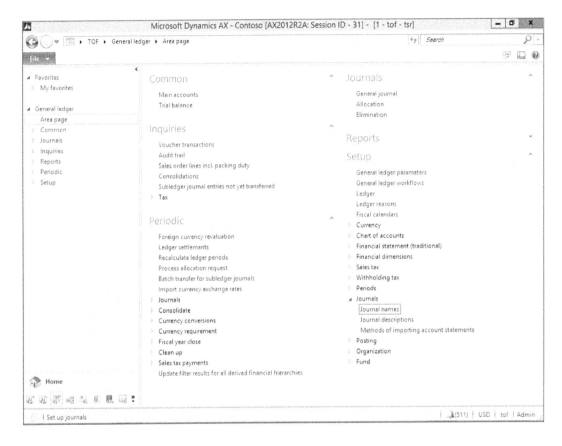

To do this, click on the **Journal Names** menu item within the **Journals** folder of the **Setup** group within the **General Ledger** area page.

Assign The Invoice Journal Workflow To The Invoice Journal

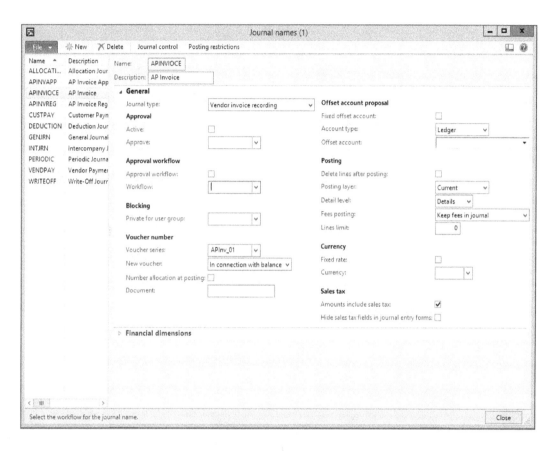

When the **Journal Names** maintenance form is displayed, select the Payables Invoice Journal that you want to attach the workflow to.

Assign The Invoice Journal Workflow To The Invoice Journal

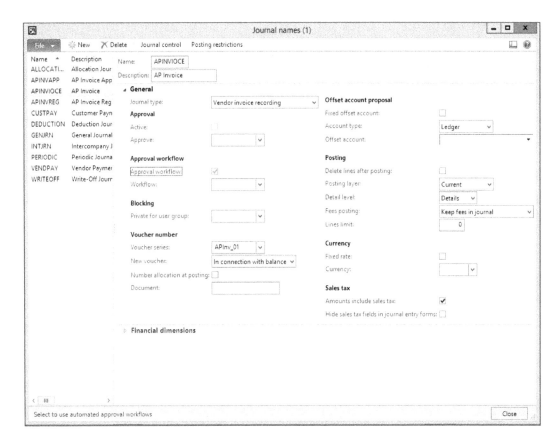

Then check the **Approval Workflow** flag.

Assign The Invoice Journal Workflow To The Invoice Journal

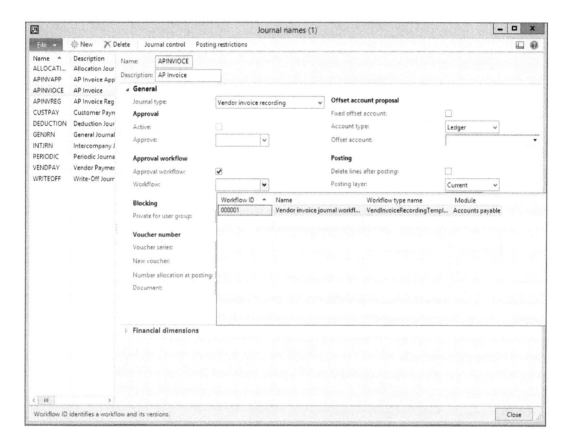

And then select the workflow that you want to attach to the journal from the **Workflow** dropdown list.

Assign The Invoice Journal Workflow To The Invoice Journal

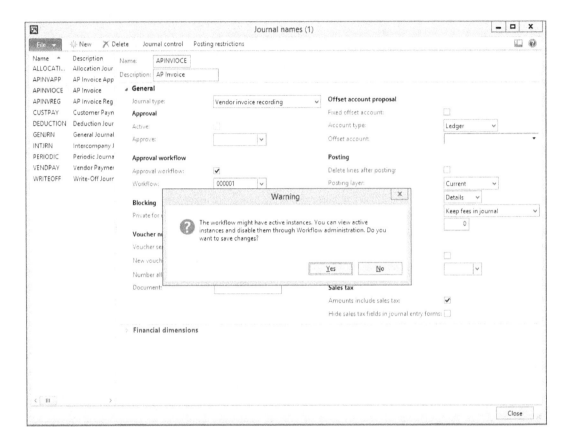

When the **Warning** dialog box is displayed, click on the **OK** button.

Assign The Invoice Journal Workflow To The Invoice Journal

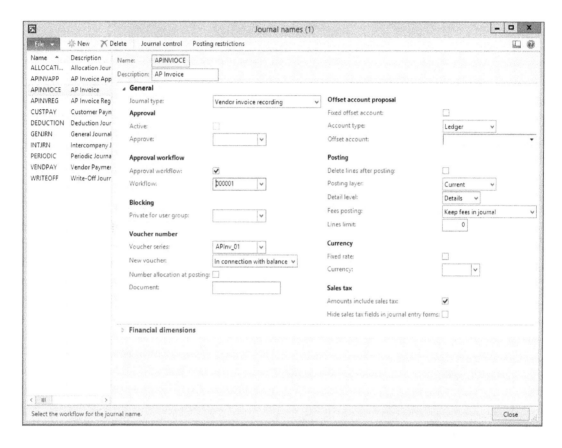

Now that you have assigned the workflow, just click on the **Close** button to exit from the form.

Submitting AP Invoice Journals For Workflow Approval

Now that we have assigned the workflow to the **Payables Invoice Journal** we can see it in action. All we need to do is create our invoice.

Submitting AP Invoice Journals For Workflow Approval

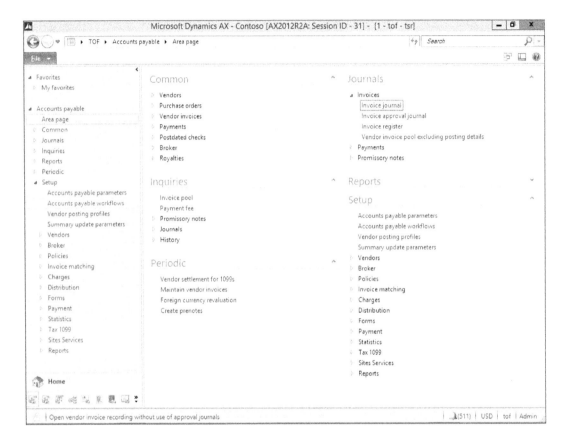

To do this, click on the **Invoice Journal** menu item within the **Invoices** folder of the **Journals** group within the **Accounts Payable** area page.

Submitting AP Invoice Journals For Workflow Approval

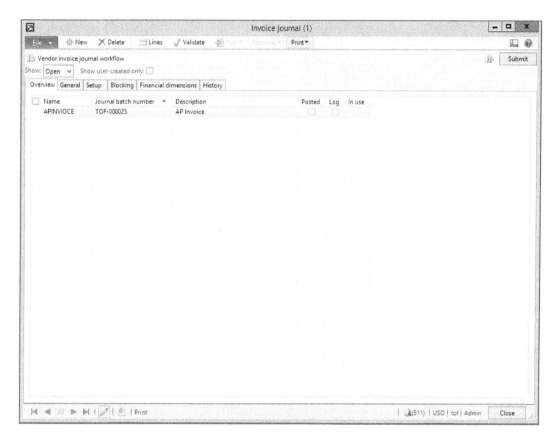

When the **Invoice Journal** list page is displayed, select any of the unposted Invoice Journals, and you will notice that the **Submit** button is displayed at the top of the form, and also that the **Post** menu item is disabled. To process the Invoice Journal just click on the **Submit** button.

Submitting AP Invoice Journals For Workflow Approval

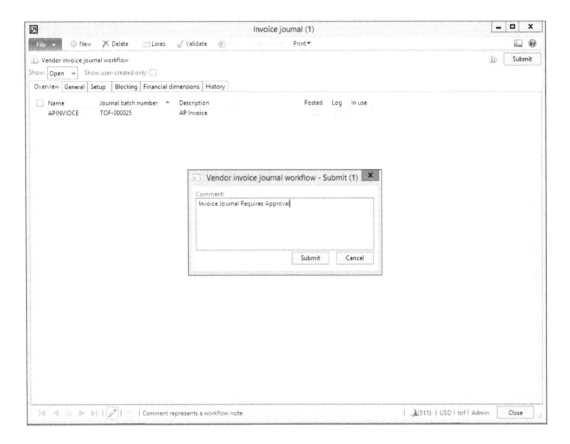

When the **Comments** dialog box is displayed, type in any notes about the Invoice Journal that you want to pass on to the approver, and then click on the **Submit** button.

Accessing Workflow Tasks Through The Work Item Notifications

There are a lot of different ways that the user is able to be notified and then access the record to approve it, but the easiest way to through the pop-up notification which gives the user real time notifications when they are assigned tasks.

Accessing Workflow Tasks Through The Work Item Notifications

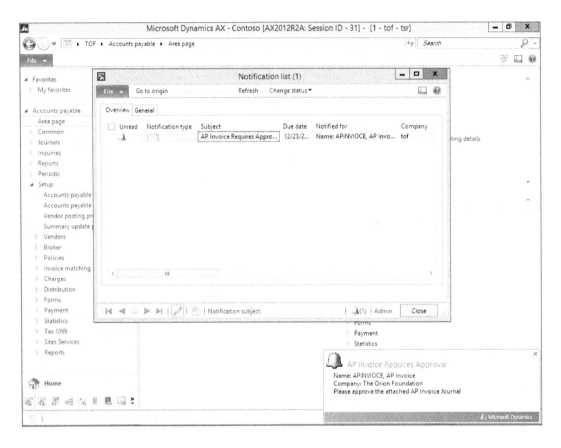

When a task is assigned to the user and they see the pop-up message that they have been assigned a workflow task, all they need to do is click on the panel.

Accessing Workflow Tasks Through The Work Item Notifications

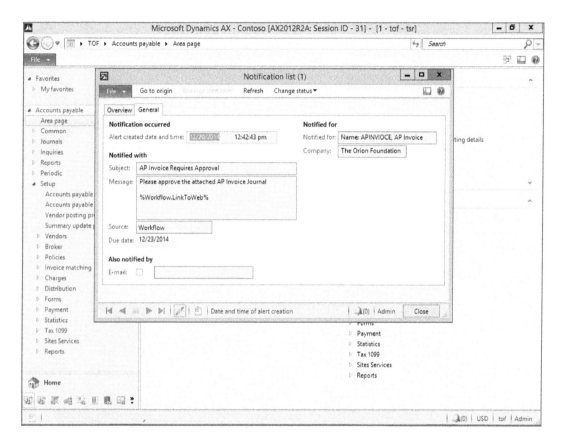

That will take them directly to the **Notification Detail** panel showing all of the details about the task.

Accessing Workflow Tasks Through The Work Item List

If users are not at their desktop at the exact time that they are assigned tasks then that's not a problem, because all of the tasks that have been assigned to them are also listed within their **Work Item List**.

Accessing Workflow Tasks Through The Work Item List

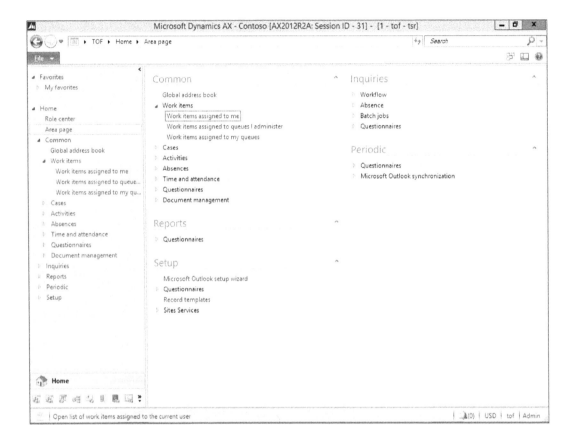

To view the users assigned tasks, click on the **Work Items Assigned To Me** menu item within the **Work Items** folder of the **Common** group of the **Home** area page.

Accessing Workflow Tasks Through The Work Item List

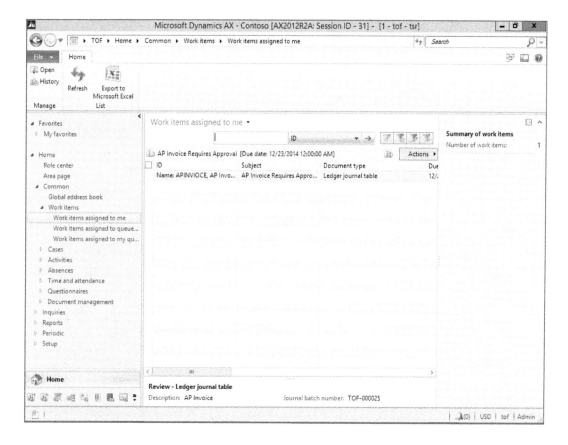

When the **Work Items Assigned To Me** list page is displayed, all of the current workflow tasks will be listed for you to work through.

Tip: To be even more organized, you can add this form to your Role Center as a Cue.

Viewing Workflow Status And History

One of the benefits of using Workflow is that all of the history of the individual workflows are tracked behind the scene. So if you ever want to see how this workflow got to where it is right now, then you can access it through the workflow history viewer.

Viewing Workflow Status And History

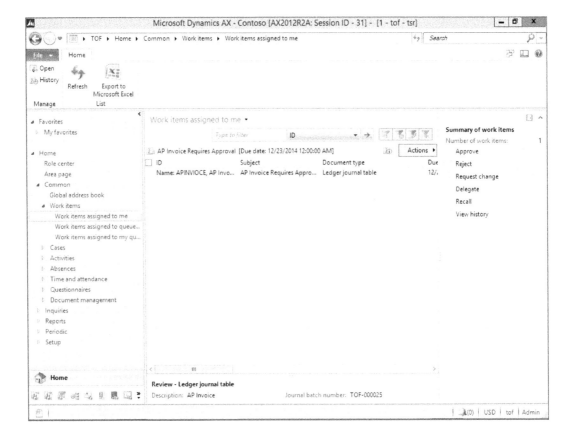

To do this, just click on the **Actions** button on any transaction that is controlled through workflow, and then click on the **View History** menu item.

Viewing Workflow Status And History

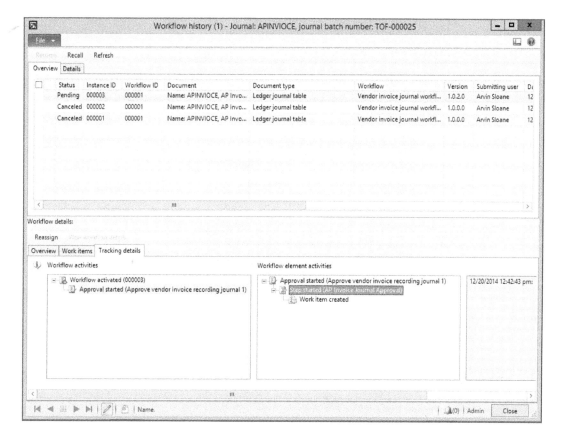

This will open up the **Workflow History** form. If you look at the bottom section of the form, and select the **Tracking Details** tab you will be able to all of the steps in the current workflow.

Approving Workflow Tasks Through The Work Item List

Now that you have been assigned a workflow task you need to **Approve** the **Payables Invoice Journal**.

Approving Workflow Tasks Through The Work Item List

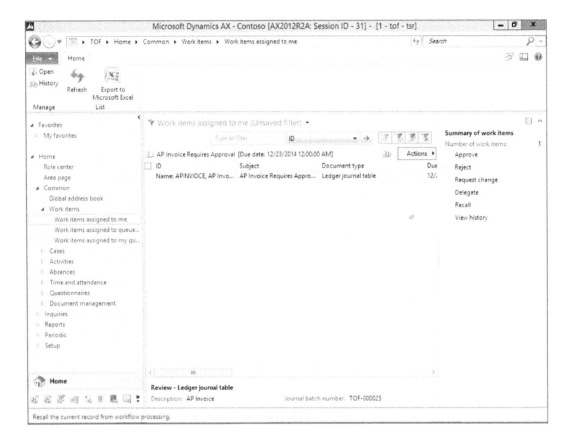

To do that, select the Invoice Journal that you have been assigned to approve, click on the **Action** button, and select the **Approve** menu item.

Approving Workflow Tasks Through The Work Item List

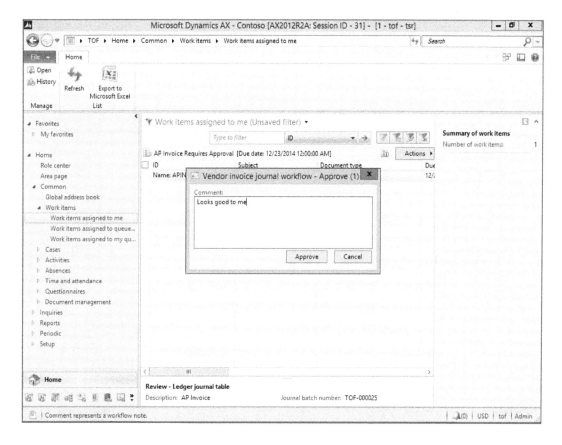

You will be asked to enter in some comments and then click the **Approve** button.

Approving Workflow Tasks Through The Work Item List

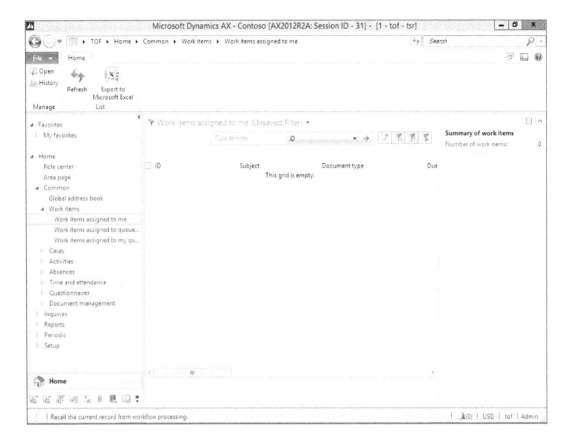

When you return back to the work item list you will also notice that the task has now been taken off your list.

Posting AP Invoice Journals After Workflow Approvals Have Been Completed

Once the **Payables Invoice Journal** has been approved, then there is one final step in the process which is to post the transaction.

Posting AP Invoice Journals After Workflow Approvals Have Been Completed

Once the workflow has completed an the journal has been approved, then you will notice that the **Post** menu item is now enabled, and you can select the **Post** option.

Adding Status Notifications To Workflows

Up until now, the only time that you are notified that there is something happening to the workflow is when you are assigned a task within the workflow process. But if you initiated the workflow process then you may want to also know when changes are made to the workflow itself so that you can see when the documents have been approved, denied, or completed. You can easily add this to the workflow process through Status Notifications.

Adding Status Notifications To Workflows

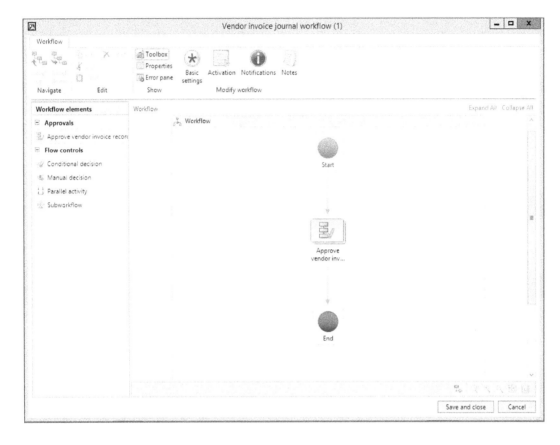

To add a status notification to a workflow, select the **Workflow** frame that surrounds the main workflow, and then click on the **Notifications** button within the **Modify Workflow** group of the **Workflow** ribbon bar.

Adding Status Notifications To Workflows

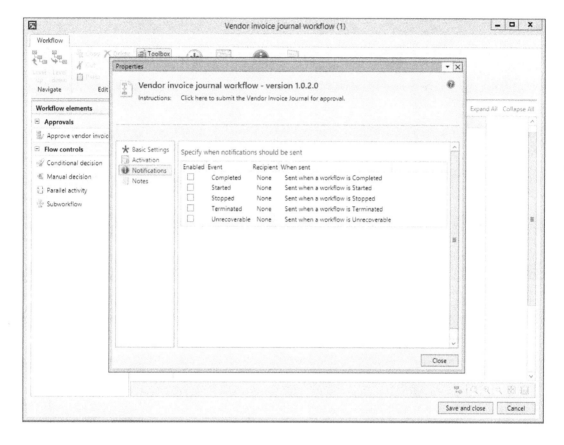

When the **Properties** form is displayed you will see all of the default scenarios for being notified.

Adding Status Notifications To Workflows

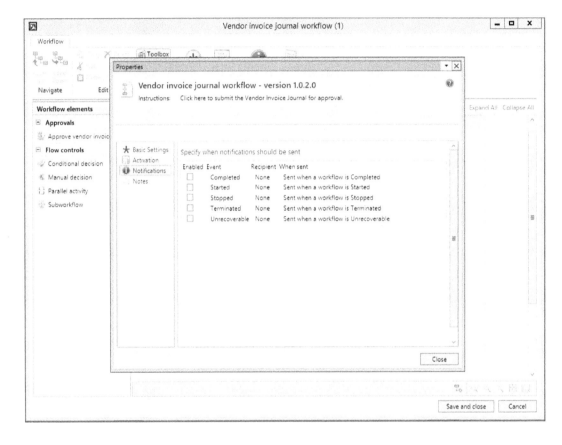

Click on the **Completed** option in order to be notified when the workflow processing has completed.

Adding Status Notifications To Workflows

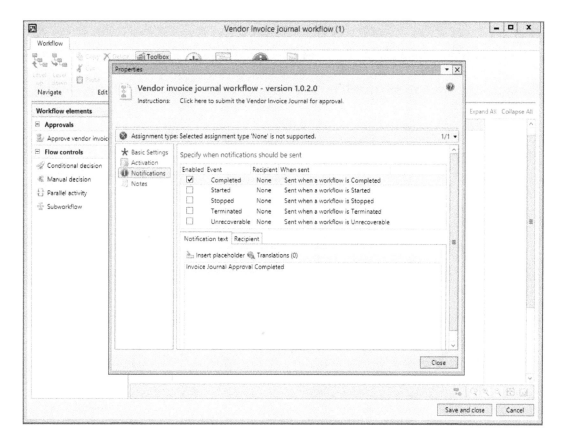

Also, if you want, you can add more text within the **Notification Text** tab.

Adding Status Notifications To Workflows

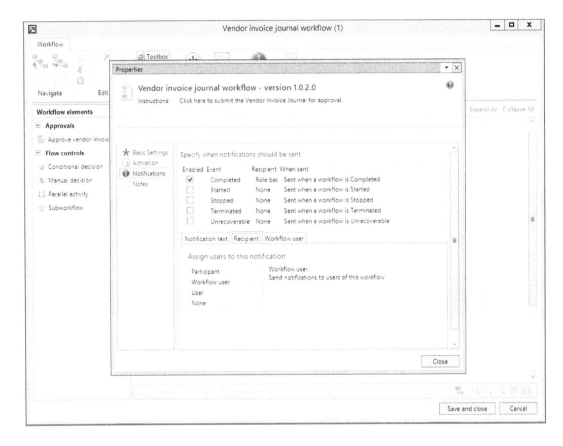

To select who is notified when the workflow is completed, switch to the **Recipient** tab and select the **Workflow User** opton.

Adding Status Notifications To Workflows

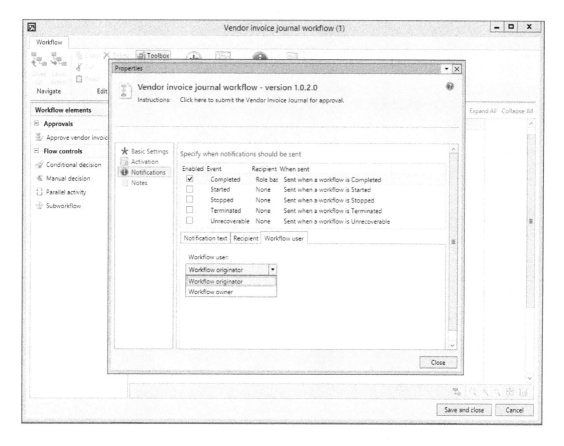

Then switch to the **Workflow User** tab, and from the **Workflow User** dropdown list, select the **Workflow Originator** option to indicate that the user that starts off the workflow should be notified.

Adding Status Notifications To Workflows

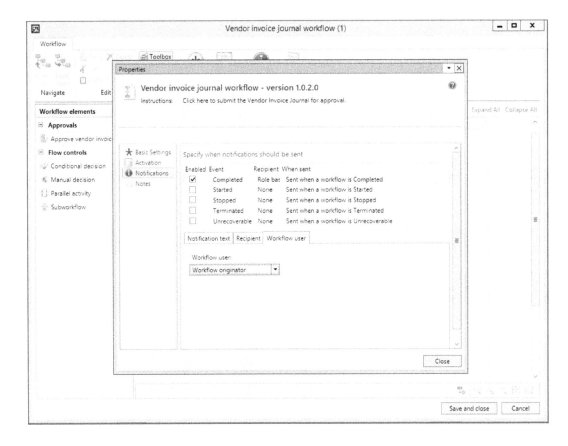

Once you have updated the notifications. You can then click on the **Close** button to exit from the form.

Publishing A New Version Of The AP Invoice Journal Approval Workflow

The workflows within **Dynamics AX** have inbuilt version control, so when you make a change to the workflow itself, in order to make it active, you need to publish and activate it as a new version.

Publishing A New Version Of The AP Invoice Journal Approval Workflow

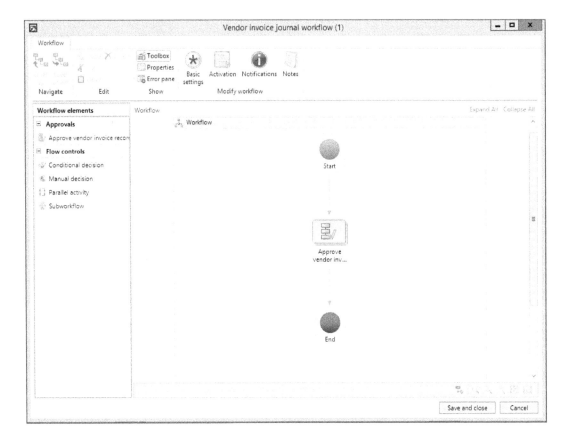

To do this, click on the **Save And Close** button on the bottom right of the workflow designer.

Publishing A New Version Of The AP Invoice Journal Approval Workflow

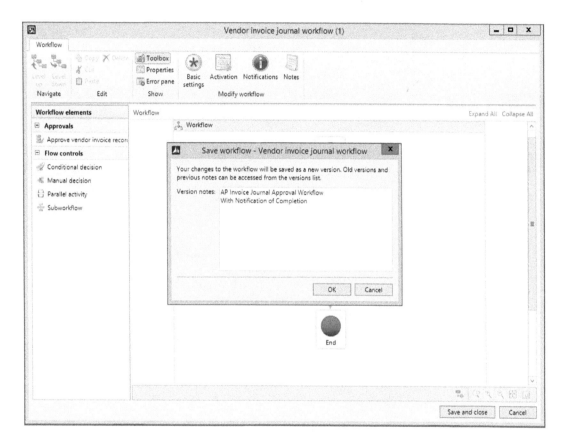

You can add additional notes here to describe what the changes are that you made to the new version and then click the **OK** button.

Publishing A New Version Of The AP Invoice Journal Approval Workflow

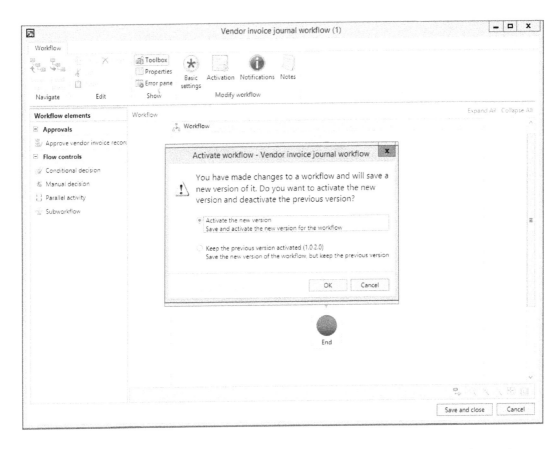

Then when the **Activation** dialog box is displayed, select the **Activate The New Version** option, and click the **OK** button.

Receiving Workflow Status Update Notifications

Once you have configured the notifications you can see it in action by submitting another **Invoice Journal** to the workflow process.

Receiving Workflow Status Update Notifications

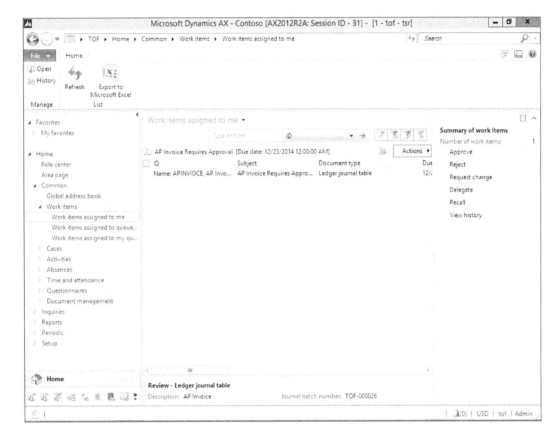

Find a **Payables Invoice Journal** that needs approval, and from the **Action** button, select the **Approve** option.

Receiving Workflow Status Update Notifications

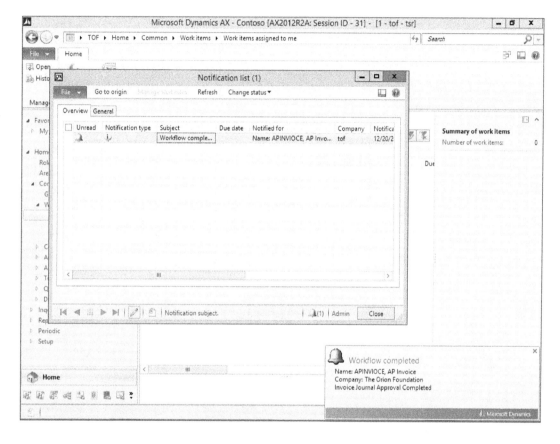

If you are the one that submitted the Invoice Journal for approval then you will receive a pop-up notification that the workflow has completed, and also you will see the notification within your **Notification List**.

Viewing Workflow Versions

As new versions of the workflows are being created, Dynamics AX does not discard the old versions. You can view all of the different versions through the workflow designer and even revert back to older versions if you find that your latest version isn't quite working how you expected it to.

Viewing Workflow Versions

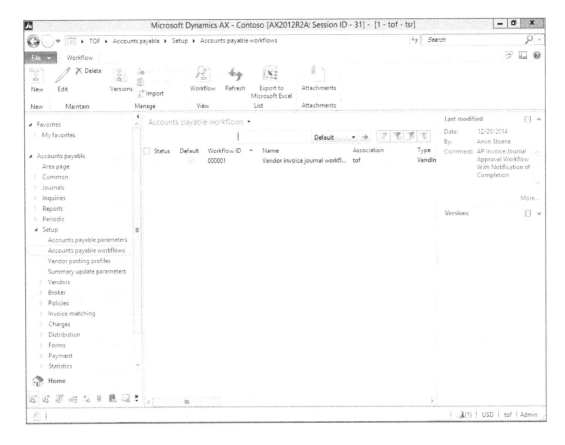

To view the versions of the workflows, open up the **Workflow** list page, select the workflow that you want to look at, and then click on the **Versions** button within the **Manage** group of the **Workflow** ribbon bar.

Viewing Workflow Versions

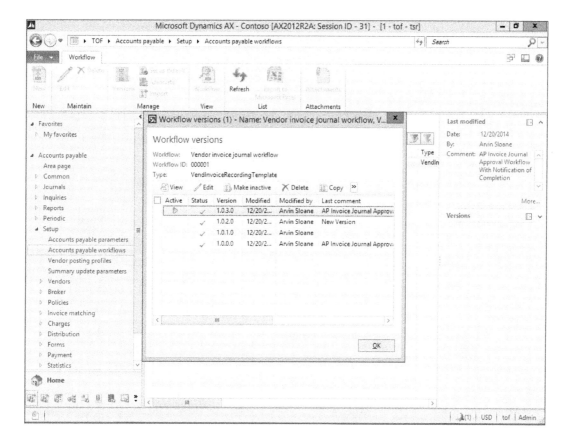

When the **Workflow Versions** list form is displayed you will see all of the versions, and are able to select older versions of the workflows.

Viewing All Workflow Statuses

As you start using workflows more you may want to see all of the workflows rather than interacting with the workflows from the transactions that they are initiated from. You can do that easily through the Workflow Statuses view within **Dynamics AX.**

Viewing All Workflow Statuses

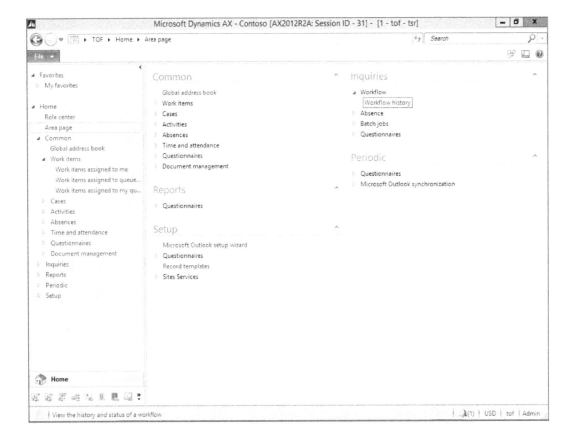

To view all of the workflows, click on the **Workflow History** menu item within the **Workflow** folder of the **Inquiries** group of the **Home** area page.

Viewing All Workflow Statuses

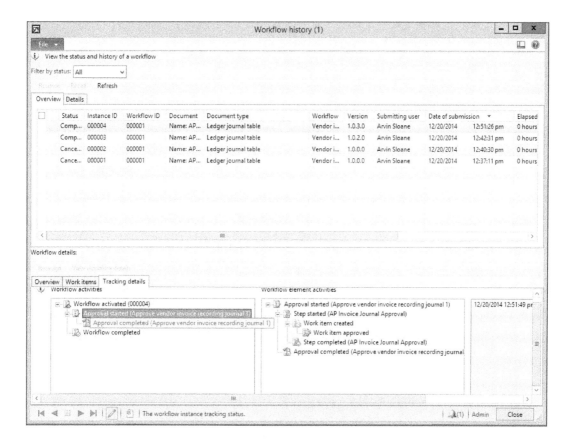

When the **Workflow History** inquiry form is displayed, you will see all of the workflows that have ran, and also that are running right now. You can view all of the processing history and details on any workflow through this inquiry.

SUMMARY

Hopefully this book has given you a good introduction to the simplest features within Dynamics AX that relate to Accounts Payable and will have shown you how to start configuring them to be used in your own implementation.

This is just a starting point for you though because there are a lot more features and functions that you may have noticed along the way that you can take advantage of.

Want More Tips & Tricks For Dynamics AX?

The Tips & Tricks series is a compilation of all the cool things that I have found that you can do within Dynamics AX, and are also the basis for my Tips & Tricks presentations that I have been giving for the AXUG, and online. Unfortunately book page size restrictions mean that I can only fit 50 tips & tricks per book, but I will create new volumes every time I reach the 50 Tip mark.

To get all of the details on this series, then here is the link:

http://dynamicsaxcompanions.com/tipsandtricks

Need More Help With Dynamics AX?

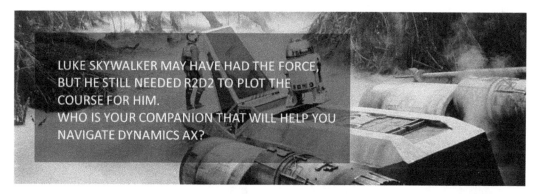

 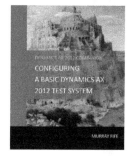  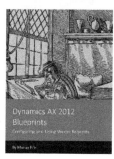

After creating a number of my walkthroughs on SlideShare showing how to configure the different areas within Dynamics AX, I had a lot of requests for the original documents so that people could get a better view of many of the screen shots and also have a easy reference as they worked through the same process within their own systems. To make them easier to access, I am in the process of moving all of the content to the Dynamics AX Companions website to easier access. If you are looking for details on how to configure and use Dynamics AX, then this is a great place for you to start.

Here is the link for the site:

http://dynamicsaxcompanions.com/

About Me

I am an author - I'm no Dan Brown but my books do contain a lot of secret codes and symbols that help guide you through the mysteries of Dynamics AX.

I am a curator - gathering all of the information that I can about Dynamics AX and filing it away within the Dynamics AX Companions archives.

I am a pitchman - I am forever extolling the virtues of Dynamics AX to the unwashed masses convincing them that it is the best ERP system in the world.

I am a Microsoft MVP - this is a big deal, there are less than 10 Dynamics AX MVP's in the US, and less than 30 worldwide.

I am a programmer - I know enough to get around within code, although I leave the hard stuff to the experts so save you all from my uncommented style.

WEB	www.murrayfife.me
	www.dynamicsaxcompanions.com
EMAIL	murray@dynamicsaxcompanions.com
TWITTER	@murrayfife
SKYPE	murrayfife
AMAZON	www.amazon.com/author/murrayfife

www.ingramcontent.com/pod-product-compliance
Lightning Source LLC
Chambersburg PA
CBHW080135060326
40689CB00018B/3794